LIFE, DEATH,
AND AFTERLIFE
IN ANCIENT EGYPT

The Djehutymose coffin in Egyptian history

3000 BC		Unification of Egypt
	Dynasties 1–2	
	Early Dynastic Period	
2500 BC	Dynasties 3–6	
	Old Kingdom	Great pyramids of Giza
	Dynasties 7–10	
	First Intermediate Period	
2000 BC	Dynasties 11–13	
	Middle Kingdom	Tale of Sinuhe composed
	Dynasties 14–16	
	Second Intermediate Period	Hyksos Invasion of Egypt
1500 BC	Dynasties 17–20	
	New Kingdom	Book of the Dead first appears
		Akhenaten and Tutankhamun ("King Tut")
		Ramesses III builds temple at Edfu
1000 BC	Dynasties 21–25	
	Third Intermediate Period	
		Period of fragmentation: Egypt ruled by Libyan and Egyptian kings (Dynasties 21–24)
		Rise in power and wealth of priesthoods
		Egypt ruled by Nubian kings (Dynasty 25)
685 BC	Dynasty 26	New indigenous dynasty of Egyptian kings from Sais
	Saite Period	Period of cultural "Renaissance"
		"Saite Recension" of Book of the Dead
625–585 BC		Death of Djehutymose, priest of Horus of Edfu
		Date of the Djehutymose coffin in the Kelsey Museum
500 BC	Dynasties 27–30	First Persian conquest of Egypt
	Late Period	
300 BC		Conquest of Egypt by Alexander the Great
	Ptolemaic Period	Egypt ruled by Macedonian-descended Ptolemies
		Ptolemaic temple at Edfu begun under Ptolemy III
30 BC		Death of Cleopatra VII and Roman takeover of Egypt

LIFE, DEATH, AND AFTERLIFE IN ANCIENT EGYPT

THE DJEHUTYMOSE COFFIN
in the Kelsey Museum of Archaeology

T. G. Wilfong

KELSEY MUSEUM PUBLICATION 9
Ann Arbor, Michigan 2013

For Janet Richards

The color photographs of the Djehutymose coffin and related artifacts in this book are by Randal Stegmeyer unless otherwise noted (see the listing of photo credits on page 112).

Published by:
Kelsey Museum of Archaeology
434 South State Street
Ann Arbor, Michigan 48109-1390
http://www.lsa.umich.edu/kelsey/research/publications

ISBN 978-0-9741873-8-9

Introduction

The Djehutymose coffin is a central part of the Kelsey Museum of Archaeology's permanent Egyptian gallery. This brightly colored artifact (dating to around 625–580 BC) is a favorite with museum visitors, a well-known landmark to University of Michigan students, and a beloved part of the Kelsey Museum's history. The coffin's vivid imagery and hieroglyphic texts inspire questions in museum visitors—questions about the coffin's purpose and making, about what the images mean, about what the texts say, about the age of the coffin, and how its materials and decoration could survive for so long. Students often see the coffin in the context of class tours and course lectures where they learn something about its wider context—how the coffin fits into the broader outlines of ancient Egyptian history, archaeology, and religion—while a few advanced students have even tackled the reading of some of the texts, learning about the complexities and ambiguities inherent in Egyptian funerary literature. The Djehutymose coffin is also a part of the history and lore of the Kelsey Museum, an ongoing presence in the lives of the faculty, staff, students, and supporters who work for the museum, and a treasure of the University of Michigan.

The Djehutymose coffin is an artifact of an ancient culture, an object with histories in both ancient and modern worlds. But it is also connected to the lives of individuals and to the wider history of the time of its making. The Djehutymose coffin can serve as a window on the lives of its owner and his family, the physical environments in which they lived, worked, died, and were buried, and the wider historical landscape of the Saite Period (664–525 BC), an important time of change in ancient Egyptian history to which this coffin bears subtle witness. Furthermore, the Djehutymose coffin reflects an entire belief system, marking a transitional point between life and afterlife and providing a glimpse into ancient Egypt's complex understanding of the landscapes traversed by the living and the dead. The coffin's ostensibly positive and hopeful images and texts betray underlying anxieties—the Egyptians' profound desire for order reflected in the Djehutymose coffin masked a deep fear of disorder; their apparent optimism about the afterlife seen in their funerary texts concealed a terror of ultimate annihilation after death. The Djehutymose coffin serves as something of a mirror of its time and context.

Fashioned nearly 2,600 years ago to contain the mummy of a man named Djehutymose, the coffin has made a complicated journey into the present. In the intervening centuries, it was separated from Djehutymose's mummy, now lost. Within the last hundred years, Djehutymose's coffin traveled far beyond the imaginings of the ancient Egyptians: from Egypt to Ann Arbor, Michigan. Donated to the University of Michigan in 1906, the coffin was long on display at the Kalamazoo Public Museum before it returned to Ann Arbor in 1989. Egyptologist Jonathan Elias studied the textual and decorative program of the coffin as part of his 1993 University of Chicago doctoral dissertation, but the Djehutymose coffin has remained otherwise unpublished except for brief descriptions in Kelsey Museum exhibition catalogues and newsletters. The aim of this book is to help explain the Djehutymose coffin in its contexts to museum visitors and to a wider audience.

The Djehutymose Coffin

The Djehutymose coffin (Kelsey Museum inventory 1989.3.1, fig. 1) consists of a lid and base, made of wood, covered with gesso, and decorated with paint and ink. It stands 72.5 inches (181.25 cm) tall, 21 inches (52.5 cm) wide at its widest point, and 21.5 inches (54 cm) deep at its deepest when the two halves are put together. The wood is probably of local Egyptian origin given its relatively low quality. Despite the quality of the wood, and the use of simple tools by the craftsmen who made it, the coffin is finely carved and well made, providing a good surface for the painted decorations that cover it.

When closed around Djehutymose's mummy, the coffin would, in effect, form an idealized image of Djehutymose as a mummy. In this state, Djehutymose is shown wearing a striped wig or headcovering, his eyes and eyebrows are outlined, his face is green, and he wears a thin, plaited false beard. The face on the coffin is not a portrait of Djehutymose as a modern viewer might understand it. To an ancient Egyptian this image would have represented Djehutymose as he would look in the afterlife, once he had become what the Egyptians knew as an *akh*, usually translated as "effective spirit." The idealized Djehutymose depicted in the coffin is calm,

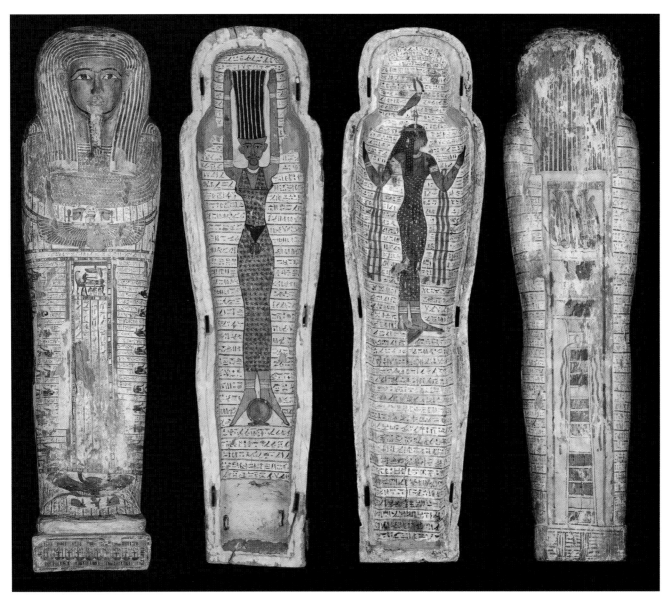

Fig. 1. The coffin of Djehutymose, c. 625–580 BC, Nag el-Hassiya, Egypt, wood, plaster, paint, ink (KM 1989.3.1): *left to right*, coffin lid exterior and interior, coffin base interior and exterior.

serene, and without worries, resembling the god Osiris with his green skin and false beard, the latter an attribute of kings, gods, and effective spirits. Djehutymose is represented by the general form of the coffin, as well as the face, head, and shoulders, but the rest of the coffin is covered with images of gods and other protective elements, as well as texts designed to protect the dead Djehutymose and get him from the point of death through judgment and into the afterlife as an effective spirit.

Who Was Djehutymose?

Contrary to what we might expect, the extensive texts on a mummy case like that of Djehutymose contain very little biographical information. All we get are the bare names and titles of Djehutymose and his parents: "Priest of Horus, Priest of the Golden One, Djehutymose, justified, son of the like-titled Nespasefy, justified, born to the mistress of the house, Tareru, justified," with minor variations. In one text on the coffin, we learn that Djehutymose's paternal grandfather was a man named Nakht-hor. Further, we know that Djehutymose had a brother named Patjenefy, also a priest. But these texts tell us nothing about where Djehutymose lived, when he was born, what he did outside of his priestly employment, or when and how he died. However, the facts we do have about Djehutymose from his coffin, along with related artifacts and parallels from other sources, provide clues that allow us to reconstruct the general outlines of his life.

The style of Djehutymose's coffin and the related artifacts allow us to situate Djehutymose and his family in the Saite Period (664–525 BC), an important time in the later history of pharaonic Egypt.[1] The Saite Period directly follows a time of political fragmentation and upheaval known as the Third Intermediate Period (1070–664 BC), when Egypt was ruled by Libyans and Nubians and briefly conquered by Assyrians. The Saite Period is also known as the 26th Dynasty (Egyptian history is divided by Egyptologists into "periods" and also organized by families or "Dynasties" of rulers), based at the northern town of Sais in the Nile Delta. The particularly long reign of its founding king, Psamtik I (often known by the Greek version of his name, Psammetichus), contributed to the overall viability of the new

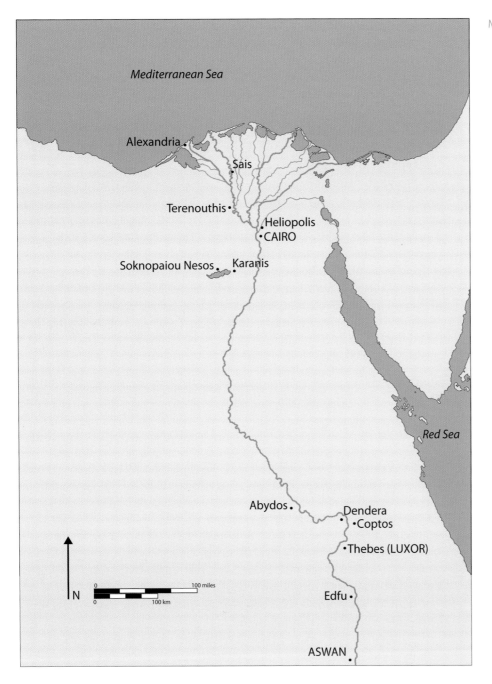

Map of ancient Egypt

Mediterranean Sea

Alexandria

Sais

Terenouthis

Heliopolis
CAIRO

Soknopaiou Nesos   Karanis

Red Sea

Abydos

Dendera
Coptos

Thebes (LUXOR)

Edfu

ASWAN

N

0   100 miles
0   100 km

Fig. 2. Funerary cone of Montuemhat, Mayor of Thebes, c. 650 BC, Western Thebes, Egypt, clay (KM 1981.4.20).

Fig. 3. Fragment of the Book of the Dead of Khamhor, containing a portion of Book of the Dead, chapter 78, c. 630 BC, Western Thebes, Egypt, papyrus, ink (KM 1981.4.25).

regime. Psamtik I ruled from 664 BC, when he reunified and took control of Egypt under Assyrian auspices, only to turn around and free Egypt from Assyrian control. By the time of his death in 610 BC, Psamtik had brought Egypt back to something approaching its former power and stability. The early Saite kings were based in the north of Egypt and consolidated their power in the south by arranging alliances with prominent Theban families (notably the adoption of Psamtik I's daughter Nitiqret by Amenirdis II, the holder of the influential Theban religious office God's Wife of Amun) and thus kept Egypt domestically peaceful.

Priestly families dominated the Saite Period, especially in and around the southern city of Thebes, and the Kelsey Museum has two artifacts relating to prominent Saite Thebans. The well-known fourth prophet of Amun and mayor of Thebes Montuemhat (who died around 650 BC), a key transitional figure in the final years of the Third Intermediate Period and beginning of the Saite Period, is represented in the Kelsey by two "funerary cones" (fig. 2). These cones, which bear Montuemhat's name and titles, were used to decorate the façade of his elaborate Theban tomb. The Kelsey also has a fragment from a Book of the Dead papyrus belonging to a distant Theban relative of Montuemhat's, a priest of the god Montu named Khamhor (who died around 630 BC) (fig. 3).[2]

The rulers of the Saite Period maintained a strong central government under a single indigenous king, and Egypt prospered economically and flourished culturally during their rule. Moreover, the Saite Period was a time of the revival and adaptation of earlier artistic styles and the reuse and revision of older religious texts, to the extent that it is sometimes referred to as the "Saite Renaissance." The reasons for this cultural "renaissance" are complex: there is a sense of adapting the past to promote the Saite rulers as true and rightful successors to the powerful earlier kings of Egypt but also of reshaping an Egyptian identity in a time of increasing foreign influence on Egyptian culture and life. This period of peace and prosperity was relatively brief in terms of Egyptian history (less than 150 years), and, in the end, the Saite rulers proved no match for growing Persian imperial ambitions. However, the stability of the Saite Period was important for providing a solid basis for Egyptian culture and society in the turbulent centuries that followed.

Djehutymose's place in the Saite Period is relatively clear. From securely dated parallels to its artistic style and certain specific features of its decoration, we know that Djehutymose's coffin was made sometime between 625 and 580 BC.[3] Thus Djehutymose would have lived and died under the reign of Psamtik I (664–610 BC) or one of his successors: Nekau II (610–595 BC), Psamtik II (595–589 BC), or Apries (589–570 BC). These kings used the domestic stability established by Psamtik I as a base for activities outside of Egypt—trade with Greece and other parts of the eastern Mediterranean as well as defensive and offensive military incursions into southwest Asia and Nubia. The military, particularly the navy, and military officials became increasingly important as the Saite Period went on, but priests still retained power and influence at centers like Thebes. Djehutymose and his family, although not directly involved in these circles of national political power, would have benefitted from the peace and prosperity of their times. So the style of Djehutymose's coffin allows us to situate him chronologically and historically, but we must turn to other evidence to find out more about the man and his family.

Fig. 4. Djehutymose's name, from the coffin lid interior.

Glyphs 1. Djehutymose's name.

Names sometimes reveal information about people's origins, occupation, or status in ancient Egypt, but they are not so helpful in the case of Djehutymose and his family. Most Egyptian personal names are made up of short sentences or phrases, often honoring gods, and the name Djehutymose means "Thoth is born" (fig. 4, glyphs 1).[4] Thus Djehutymose's name honors the god Thoth, the ibis-headed Egyptian god associated with writing who functioned as scribe to the gods. The cult of Thoth had a major center in the Egyptian city of Hermopolis, but the use of Thoth's name does not imply any local associations. Djehutymose was a popular name in ancient Egypt thanks to the four kings who had the name in the 18th Dynasty (their name usually being rendered Thutmose). In particular, Thutmose III (c. 1479–1425 BC) was the likely inspiration for the popularity of the name: this king was known long after his death for his extensive military exploits and empire-building, and his name would have had particular resonance in the history-conscious Saite Period. So, rather than specifically honoring a local god, our Djehutymose more likely got his name as a result of the ongoing popularity of a military king of nearly 700 years earlier, and the name provides no clues as to our coffin owner's origin or status. The names of Djehutymose's relatives are likewise unhelpful in this regard, but fortunately their titles are much more informative.

Djehutymose, his father Nespasefy, and his brother Patjenefy all bear the titles "Priest of Horus," sometimes written more fully as "Priest of

Fig. 5. Djehutymose's full name and titles and father's name and titles, from the coffin lid interior.

Horus of Edfu," and "Priest of the Golden One" (fig. 5). These titles identify the men as priests at the temple of Horus of Edfu, so we know that the family would have lived in the town of Edfu. Priests formed part of the small, literate elite of Egyptian society, so Djehutymose would have been relatively well-to-do, although not a member of the highest elite. The name Djehutymose was relatively common at Edfu, as were Nespasefy and Patjenefy, and it has not been possible to link our family with any known individuals of these names. Edfu was a significant city in the south of Egypt but not as important as nearby Thebes, a major southern religious and political center with which many Edfuans had ties. Djehutymose's father, Nespasefy, is also twice identified as "Priest of Heliopolis," an important city in the north associated with the cults of sun-gods. Nespasefy's title may have simply been honorary, but it may also have indicated actual priestly duties in Heliopolis that would have required travel. Either way, the family's primary connections were with Edfu: most of their work was there, and Edfu would have been their home. Although Djehutymose and his family may have been provincials, they had ties elsewhere and were relatively prosperous in their provincial base.

In their offices of Priest of Horus and Priest of the Golden One, Djehutymose, his father, and his brother would have participated in the many ritual activities and festivals of the temple of Horus of Edfu. Horus was the son of the goddess Isis, posthumously fathered by the god Osiris and central to Egyptian mythology and kingship, so the temple of Horus at Edfu was a major site of worship and pilgrimage. The temple that Djehutymose worked in was begun in the New Kingdom under Ramesses III (c. 1184–1153 BC) and elaborated on afterwards, but this temple was ultimately replaced by the magnificent temple built in the Ptolemaic Period (332–30 BC) at Edfu, one of the best-preserved Egyptian temples to survive into the present (fig. 6).[5] The Temple of Horus had a relationship to the temple of Hathor at Dendera (fig. 7), thanks to the "marriage" of Horus of Edfu and Hathor of Dendera, celebrated in an annual festival between the two temples that, effectively, provided "conjugal visits" between the cult images of the two deities. The goddess Hathor was associated with pleasure, sexuality, and fertility, and her festivals were often celebrated by drunkenness. Hathor is, in fact, the "Golden One" of Djehutymose's titles, and the fact that Djehutymose was priest of both Horus and Hathor may indicate his particular involvement in their joint festivals or other connections to the Dendera temple.

6

7

Beyond this annual festival, Djehutymose's priestly duties would have tended more toward the maintenance of the daily cult of Horus.[6] Each temple held a cult image of its god, a small statue made of gold or silver and decorated with other precious materials that was "activated" by a special ceremony to make it a suitable home for the god. The daily ritual surrounding the cult image was central to the activities of the temple. Priests awakened the statue in the morning, removed it from its shrine, washed and clothed it, and gave it offerings. The statue was then ready to take part in ritual activities throughout the day, sometimes carried by priests in a special barque, or boat-shrine, while surrounded by the recitation of hymns and prayers, chanted and accompanied by the sistrum, a sacred rattle. In the evening, priests would again make offerings to the statue, unclothe and wash it, and then put it to "bed" by closing it into its shrine. The priests would awaken the statue again in the morning, and the whole ritual would be repeated daily. A priest of the temple of Horus of Edfu may have participated in any or all of these ritual activities; he may also have been involved in temple administration, supervision of the many temple employees, or work in the temple library involving the maintenance, copying, and writing of sacred texts. Priests were expected to follow many regulations of conduct

Fig. 6. David Roberts, "Temple of Edfu: Ancient Apollinopolis, Upper Egypt," 1856, lithograph (private collection).

Fig. 7. David Roberts, "View from under the Portico of the Temple of Dendera," 1856, lithograph (private collection).

Fig. 8. Stela of She-
damenemope of-
fering to a ram god,
282 BC, Naucratis,
Egypt, limestone,
paint (KM 25803).

Fig. 9. Decorated
cat mummy, Early
Roman Period, 1st
century AD, cat
remains, cloth, paint
(KM 1971.2.183).

while carrying out their daily duties. Inscriptions in the Ptolemaic temple of Horus of Edfu list many of these requirements and regulations for priests, including not being unclean, not lying, not stealing from the temple, not running in sandals, not speaking loudly to other priests, and not getting drunk in the temple.[7] The temple was literally the house and home of the god: its priests were expected to behave with respect and dignity.

Djehutymose, his father, and his brother would have observed the regulations specific to their temple, and each would have had his appointed tasks in the life of the temple involving at least some of the duties listed above. Djehutymose's brother Patjenefy is also given an additional title, "Overseer of the Mysteries of Horus of Edfu," which indicates that he had extra duties. This title suggests that Patjenefy was connected to the animal cult at Edfu. Many Egyptian gods had specific associations with animals, and the temples of these gods would often feature cults around the gods' animals.[8] For larger animals, like the Buchis bull of Armant or the Apis bull of Memphis, a single animal would be chosen based on markings and other characteristics and treated as the embodiment of the god. The chosen animal participated in rituals, oracles, and other cult activities; it would receive a lavish burial on its natural death and be succeeded by another animal (fig. 8). For smaller animals the practice was often different: a temple would be home to hundreds, if not thousands, of the animals related to its god. Priests would choose one animal from this group annually to act as the representative of the god in rituals, while the other animals would either roam the temple or be caged or penned together. The temple of the cat-goddess Bastet at Bubastis, for example, was known for the many cats that roamed the temple, and temples of the crocodile gods in the Fayum kept crocodiles in pools. Not all of the smaller animals kept in this way would die a natural death, though: at some animal temples, for a price, an animal could be killed, mummified, and left as a special offering in the crypt of the temple (fig. 9). This was an act that would have seemed less disrespectful to an ancient Egyptian than to us—the animal was essentially being sent back to its god to bring a message from the person who paid for it to be killed and embalmed.

Thus, the Horus temple at Edfu would have contained a cage of falcons (or similar but smaller birds of prey), from which one bird would be chosen annually and crowned in a special ceremony to act as representative of Horus of Edfu. The remaining birds could be made into mummies

    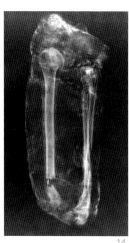

as offerings. Djehutymose's brother Patjenefy would have been involved in this animal cult of Horus of Edfu. Although his title ultimately identifies him with Anubis, the god of embalming, Patjenefy would not have done the actual work of embalming the bird mummies. He would have been connected to the part of the cult that dealt with the mummification of the birds and would have supervised the ritual wrapping of the mummies after embalming. The Kelsey Museum has three mummies of small birds of prey that could have come from the Edfu cult (figs. 10–11). In all three of these bird mummies, the beaks or parts of their heads are left visible through their wrappings, and this may have been done deliberately as a guarantee of the mummies' authenticity (fig. 12). Documents from the Ptolemaic Period attest to corruption in the animal cults, which is also suggested by surviving animal-shaped mummies that do not contain appropriate animal remains. The Kelsey Museum, for example, has a baboon-shaped mummy that contains human arm bones, as revealed in X-rays (figs. 13–14). We will hope that Djehuytmose's brother Patjenefy was not involved in these dishonest activities, but his additional title of "Overseer of the Mysteries of Horus of Edfu" almost certainly resulted in higher status and a greater income for Patjenefy (a possibility also suggested by a piece of his funerary equipment described below).

There was relatively little social mobility in ancient Egypt, and successive generations in families tended to have the same occupation. Given the fact that Djehutymose and his father and brother were priests, we can

Fig. 10. Bird mummy, Ptolemaic–Early Roman Periods, 332 BC–AD 100, bird remains, cloth, pitch (KM 1971.2.181).

Fig. 11. Bird mummy, side view of fig. 10.

Fig. 12. Bird mummy, close-up, Ptolemaic–Early Roman Periods, 332 BC–AD 100, bird remains, cloth, pitch (KM 1971.2.182).

Fig. 13. Baboon mummy, Ptolemaic–Early Roman Periods, 332 BC–AD 100, human arm bones, cloth, pitch (KM 88822).

Fig. 14. Baboon mummy: x-ray (by James Harris).

safely assume that his grandfather Nakht-hor (whose name means "Horus is strong") was a priest at the same temple. Djehutymose's sons, if he had any, would have been priests as well. We do not know whether Djehutymose was married and had children: it would have been expected of a man of his class and occupation and unusual for him to remain unmarried past the age of 20 or so. Djehutymose is likely to have married a woman from another Edfu priestly family, possibly someone from a distant branch of his own. Djehutymose's mother, Tareru, is given the title *nebet per*, usually translated "mistress of the house." This title, often borne by elite women in ancient Egypt, carried with it a wide range of activities and responsibilities.[9] Tareru would have been responsible for the administration of an elite household with servants, supervising the domestic production of bread and beer as well as ordinary cooking, dealing with the household finances along with supervising the care of all children and the education of female children, and possibly even administering any farmland that the family owned. Djehutymose's wife, if he had one, would have done the same thing in, ideally, a separate household. Extended families in a single household were not uncommon but not necessarily seen as ideal given the problems that could emerge.

The women in Djehutymose's family would have had theoretical legal equality with the men, but there were in practice many things that women could not or did not do. Gender roles were more socially enforced than legally mandated in ancient Egypt. Still, Djehutymose's mother or putative wife could have owned and farmed (or, more likely, hired others to farm) her own land, could have owned moveable property disposable in any way she saw fit, and would have had greater autonomy than women in other ancient Mediterranean cultures. Few occupations outside the household were open to women, however, and Djehutymose's female relatives would have been most actively involved in home administration and childcare, almost certainly with the help of servants. Given the high rates of infant and child mortality, as well as high rates of women dying in childbirth, the birth of children came at a cost, even in the elite priestly circles in which Djehutymose lived. Djehutymose's own parents had at least two sons, but there may have been more children, and it is impossible to know how many children Djehutymose himself might have had.

Beyond their jobs and home life, Djehutymose and his family would have been involved in other activities. Although they were priests, it is likely that they participated in Egypt's dominant economic endeavor of agriculture in some way, as did nearly everyone in ancient Egypt regardless of class. Djehutymose's family would have owned or rented agricultural land and hired farmers to work it, growing grain and produce and selling any surplus.[10] Otherwise, the local temple and its elaborate calendar of festivals that punctuated the year would have dominated their lives. Even when not "working," Djehutymose and his family would have participated in temple events, and the many festivals would have provided entertainment and activity within the community. Aside from work, ancient Egyptians understood "leisure" very differently than we do now. Most sports and physical activity were associated with either children or the poor in ancient Egypt and would have held little appeal for the elites of Djehutymose's time. Sporting activities that were suitable for the elites, such as fishing, fowling and hunting, might have been too elite for the provincial priests of Edfu—these pastimes were normally associated with kings and very high officials. Formal entertainment activities were limited. "Professional" music and theater resided firmly in the temples and were religious in nature: the temple at Edfu in the Ptolemaic Period was host to an elaborate series of mystical dramas about the god Horus. These performances were probably already in practice much earlier and may have been seen by Djehutymose and his family. Otherwise, formal theater as such was unknown in ancient Egypt, but the informal oral performance of Egyptian literature, with its tales of adventure and magic, would have provided entertainment. Informal music could be had from itinerant musicians, such as the groups of female musicians and dancers described in literature and represented in party scenes in tombs of the New Kingdom. Indeed, most of the entertainment of Djehutymose and his family would have been social—parties and gatherings of family, colleagues, and friends. The Egyptians' fondness for parties and feasts, especially among the elite Egyptians who could best afford them, is well attested, and if some had a religious or even funerary basis, they could still be enjoyable.

Even in the midst of a festive party, Egyptians were reminded of the inevitability of death. Egyptian harpers' songs raised the subject at the parties where the harpers entertained, while Classical authors about Egypt refer to an Egyptian custom of bringing out a coffin or image of a dead person at the end of a feast as a reminder of the partiers' mortality.[11] Perhaps Djehutymose's own coffin can serve as a symbol for the coffin at the feast, as

Fig. 15. Idealized image of Djehutymose from lid exterior of coffin.

it raises the question of Djehutymose's death (fig. 15). The coffin itself cannot answer some of the basic questions we will have: how did Djehutymose die, and how old was he when he died? If we had Djehutymose's mummy, these questions might be easily answered. Although cause of death can be difficult to determine from mummified remains, obvious injuries and general information about health can be clear, while the age at death can be fairly easy to guess for adult mummies. But Djehutymose's mummy was long ago separated from his coffin and is now lost; there is little other information available. The texts on coffins never make reference to these points, and it is unusual for any sort of textual evidence from Djehutymose's time to record a cause of death. It is not until the Graeco-Roman Period that records of causes of death and ages at death become common, thanks to recordkeeping practices largely foreign to Egypt. Indeed, data from the Roman census in Egypt has yielded an enormous amount of demographic information that can permit us to talk about average ages at death and mortality; although coming from hundreds of years after Djehutymose's death, this later census data can at least suggest some useful possibilities, especially as lifespans tend to increase across time.[12]

It is an often-repeated "fact" that the average lifespan of a man in ancient Egypt was 25, and as a mathematical average this may technically be more or less correct. But this does not mean that Djehutymose would have begun preparing his coffin at age 24. Average ages in ancient Egypt are heavily skewed by the high rates of infant and child mortality: an estimated one of every three children died before the age of one in Roman Egypt, and one of every four of those who survived the age of one would have died before the age of five. There was considerable risk through the later years of childhood as well. Given his priestly titles, we know that Djehutymose survived these dangerous childhood years to become an adult.

Another clear indication that Djehutymose died after childhood is found in the size of his coffin itself: his likely height as suggested by the height of the cavity for his body in his coffin. This cavity is 5' 7" (170.0 cm); if we allow a few inches for mummy wrappings, but also factor in an inch or two for shrinkage of the body from mummification, we might arrive at a height in life of 5' 5" (165.0 cm) or 5' 6" (167.5 cm). A comprehensive survey of heights from skeletal remains of Egyptians from the Predynastic Period to the Middle Kingdom (c. 5000–1800 BC) gives the average height for adult males in Egypt over that long period as 5' 4"–5' 7" (162.9–169.6 cm).[13]

During this period, the average height of an adult male did not increase dramatically, and there are no indications that average height increased significantly over the thousand years or so before Djehutymose's time. The size of the coffin cavity shows that Djehutymose would fall squarely into the average height of an adult male, confirming the already strong likelihood found in the other evidence that he was an adult.

Even adulthood was fraught with dangers in ancient Egypt, especially for the great majority of the population who were poor farmers doing manual labor. Death from work-related injuries and violence were much more common than in the modern Western world. Although medicine in ancient Egypt was advanced in comparison with that of other ancient Mediterranean cultures, understandings of disease and infection were still very limited. Egyptian doctors could effectively treat a variety of injuries and diseases, but many conditions that are seen as minor inconveniences in our world would have been fatal to ancient Egyptians. Djehutymose, as a member of a relatively leisured elite, would have had a much better chance of survival than most Egyptians, with better nutrition, better living and working conditions, and better access to such medical care as existed. Being a man also was a factor in Djehutymose's favor: women's mortality in childbearing years would have been higher than that of men at comparable ages, even for elites. In general, if a man survived past childhood, an overall lifespan of 45 to 50 years was likely, ages into the 50s not uncommon, and ages into the 60s and even 70s were not unknown. Thus Djehutymose, assuming he had no fatal accidents or catastrophic illnesses, could have lived into his 40s or 50s, or beyond.

Fig. 16. Heart scarab, back view, 25th–26th Dynasty, c. 747–525 BC, serpentine (KM 1981.4.77).

Fig. 17. Heart scarab, inscription on base of fig. 16.

Djehutymose in a Family Burial

Whatever his age, at the point of death Djehutymose would have entered into a uniquely Egyptian process of embalming known as mummification, a process for which the Egyptians were recognized throughout the ancient world. Thanks to both the ancient evidence and modern scientific investigation of mummies, we now have a good understanding of this once mysterious process.

After Djehutymose's death, his body would have been taken to the local embalmers, technicians who performed the messy physical processes of embalming along with priests who performed the necessary rituals.[14] Djehutymose's body would have been cleaned and probably, given his priestly status, entirely shaved. Egyptian processes of embalming involved preservation through drying, requiring the removal of as much liquid and "wet" material from the body as possible. The first steps in this process entailed the draining of fluids from the body and then the removal of the internal organs. The embalmers removed the brain through the nose or an incision in the neck and disposed of it without special treatment (the brain was not seen as important in ancient Egypt). Organs from the body cavity were typically removed through an incision and treated separately—dried and wrapped in packages, the organs were either placed in specific types of containers (canopic jars) or returned to the body after embalming was complete. (Both approaches are found in the Saite Period when Djehutymose lived.) The reason for the removal of internal organs was partly practical— they are typically the first parts of the body to decay—but also symbolic: the removed organs would be needed in the afterlife and were placed under the protection of specific gods and goddesses. Only the heart remained in place, again for reasons both practical and religious: largely muscle, the heart is not particularly quick to decay, but it was also normally left in the body for its own protection. Ancient Egyptians considered the heart to be the seat of intelligence and memory and crucial to the afterlife survival of the dead person. The heart would be called upon to testify on the dead person's behalf in a final judgment, and the body cavity was the safest place for it. Amulets known as heart scarabs were sometimes placed in the chest cavity near the heart as both protector and backup in case the actual heart was damaged or lost (figs. 16–17). Once the embalmers had eviscerated Djehutymose's body, the long process of drying began in earnest. The embalmers placed the body under heaps of natron, a mineral compound rather like a mixture of salt and baking soda that naturally occurs in the Egyptian desert. The natron would both dry out the body and help remove any smell from it. This drying could be accomplished in 40 days but might take longer, and indeed the length of the overall process could vary depending on the economic status of the deceased.[15]

Meanwhile, other preparations for Djehutymose's burial were necessary; the entire embalming process would take 40 to 70 days, so all other work had to be done in that period. Most important was the construction and decoration of Djehutymose's coffin, which was made after his death. In the Saite Period the coffin was the most important item for a burial after the mummy and perhaps almost as expensive as the embalming process. Djehutymose's coffin was probably made at a local workshop, but one experienced in the making of funerary equipment. The craftsmen used local Egyptian wood instead of the more expensive (and finer quality) imported cedar (fig. 18). The lid and base of Djehutymose's coffin were carved in single pieces from individual tree trunks, but an additional element (the foot of the lid) had to be made separately and pegged on, as the piece of wood was not big enough for the entire coffin lid. Craftsmen would have roughed out the general shape of the coffin and then carried out the finer carving, all of this accomplished with relatively simple bronze saws, chisels, and other tools. The six wooden tenons eventually used to fasten the coffin shut were pegged into slots in the edge of the lid before the coffin was decorated. (These tenons would fit into corresponding slots in the coffin base.) The foot was also attached with tenons and pegs at this point. (Figure 19 shows both foot tenons and side holes.) The craftsmen filled the peg holes, joins, and any pits or imperfections, covered the coffin with gesso and sanded down the surface to provide a smooth ground for the addition of paint.

Next, an anonymous artist laid out the designs and figures on the blank gesso surface in light red lines.[16] He then painted in areas of color, and, as a final step, he laid down outlines in black. The speed with which this work needed to be done required a somewhat quick, cursive style but was aided by the Egyptian canon of proportions, which allowed easy reproduction of standardized figures on a grid from a master copy. In only rare cases do we see digressions from canonical style, but these are illuminating insights into the artist's work. The full-length figure of the sky-goddess Nut on the underside of the coffin lid posed a special challenge. Egyptian

Fig. 18. Exposed wood on the Djehutymose coffin, showing the grain.

Fig. 19. View of tenons used to attach coffin foot to lid.

Fig. 20. The goddess Amentet, showing classical, canonical style.

Fig. 21. The goddess Nut, showing less traditional, full-face representation style.

20

21

22

23

24

Fig. 22. Portion of Book of the Dead, chapter 89, inscribed in color.

Fig. 23. Example of hieroglyphs written with a fine pen on the smooth exterior of the Djehutymose coffin.

Fig. 24. Example of sign (on right) resembling cursive hieratic script.

artistic traditions dictate certain conventions for representing the human figure in two-dimensional art: parts of the body are shown from different perspectives that represent ideal views. Thus, in a canonical representation of a human face, the face itself is shown in profile, from the side, as is the mouth, but the eyes, eyebrows, and ears are shown as if from the front, as can be seen in the figure of the goddess Amentet in the interior of the coffin base (fig. 20). But the figure of Nut would be directly above the mummy when the coffin was closed, and such images of Nut are often shown full face, as if the goddess would be looking directly into the eyes of the dead person. Egyptian artists were relatively unused to depicting such non-canonical full-face representations, though, and the artist's inexperience in drawing in this way shows in the slightly uncertain symmetry of the two halves of the face, as well as the positioning and detail of the arms and the breasts (fig. 21). Far from being a flaw (at least, to modern eyes), the artist's inexperience resulted in a rendering of a full-faced Nut that is vivid and striking, full of character and individuality.

Once the figures were fully painted on the coffin, then a scribe would add the inscriptions in ink. One inscription, the five lines of text in the lower center of the coffin lid, had already been drawn in red and blue paint by the artist who did the decoration (fig. 22),[17] but the majority of the texts on the coffin were written in black ink by a scribe (fig. 23). Djehutymose's coffin is covered in texts, and the scribe had to copy these from a master text on papyrus. The texts are inscribed in hieroglyphs—the picture writing used for formal texts and inscriptions—although the original master text may have been at least partly written in the cursive form of Egyptian script known as hieratic (there are a few hieratic-style signs among the hieroglyphs that suggest this) (fig. 24). The hieroglyphs themselves are often abbreviated and not the fully drawn out signs one might find on a monumental stone inscription: again, the coffin makers were working against the deadline of Djehutymose's approaching funeral. The scribe used a fine pen for the texts on the relatively smooth outside of the coffin but a thicker pen or brush on the rougher surfaces of the interior that could have splintered a finer pen (fig. 25). The handwriting on the exterior may be somewhat abbreviated but is generally quite fine and practiced. The handwriting on the interior is a different matter: the scribe had to contend not only with a coarser pen or brush and a rougher surface but also with awkward curved surfaces and even more awkward interior edges. The text in the interior has more copying errors than that on the exterior, possibly also due to the difficulties of writing there. The scribe caught and corrected some errors as he worked, but there seems to have been a final proofreading when other errors were corrected by insertions above the line of text (fig. 26). Once the coffin was fully painted and inscribed, it would have been covered with a clear varnish, of which discolored drops of excess varnish are now visible in some places on the coffin (fig. 27).

Other preparations would take place alongside the manufacture of the coffin: any wooden objects for the burial—statues, stelae (memorial tablets), chests, or other items—may have been made in the same workshop as the coffin, probably by the same craftsmen and painters. Items that required different processes—ceramics or objects of the fired mineral compound known as faience—would be made by different specialists. Small faience objects such as shabtis (mummiform servant figures) or amulets would be mass-produced in molds, in some cases customized for the deceased. In earlier eras, the embalming period was also a time for the preparation or completion of an elaborately decorated tomb, but this was no longer common practice. In effect, the images and texts once placed on the tomb walls

Fig. 25. Example of hieroglyphs written (with difficulty) with brush on rough interior of coffin.

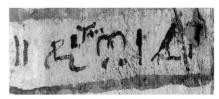

Fig. 26. Correction of an error: omitted text inserted above line on coffin base interior.

Fig. 27. Visible drips of excess varnish on coffin exterior.

were now placed on the coffin. Although very high elites in the Saite Period still built elaborate funerary monuments (such as the extensive Theban tomb of the prominent official Montuemhat), provincial elites like Djehutymose's family would have had simple, undecorated tombs, and relatively little would have had to be done if there was already an existing family tomb. The family would have taken care of the logistical arrangements for Djehutymose's funeral—catering, hiring of mourners, arranging for officiating priests—during the embalming period.

Once Djehutymose's body had fully dried out, the embalmers took it from the natron for further treatment. To counteract the drying of Djehutymose's skin and resulting brittleness, the embalmers would have anointed his body with expensive perfumed oils. Such oils served ritual, protective functions and demonstrated family wealth but also served emollient and cosmetic purposes: the oils would soften and smooth the dried skin, and their perfumes would help hide any residual smell of decay in the body.[18] To counteract signs of emaciation, the treated body might also be packed with sawdust or other material, inserted under the skin to restore sunken cheeks and other bodily contours, although this had become less common by the Saite Period. Artificial eyes might be put in place, the eyes and brows might be lined in makeup, and the skin might even be painted; jewelry and amulets could then be placed on the body. Once the body was fully prepared, it was wrapped in linen bandages in a carefully prescribed order: fingers and toes, then arms and legs would be wrapped separately, then bound together to form the classic mummy shape, while the wrapping of the head and body would be carefully performed to protect the body as well as preserve its form. The amount and quality of cloth used was a clear indicator of status: elite mummies tended to use large amounts of expensive fine linen, and the bulk and heaviness of the resulting mummy would subtly show off family wealth. Priests performed the wrapping as a ritual, reciting prayers as they worked and inserting amulets at appropriate points in the bandages. As a finishing touch, the outer bandages would often be "sealed" with pitch or resin: the base of Djehutymose's coffin shows traces of pitch or resin that has stuck to the interior (fig. 28). Once the mummy was fully wrapped, it was appropriately decorated, often in this period with cartonnage—cloth strengthened and smoothed with plaster and gesso, then painted and sometimes even gilded. Most visible would be the cartonnage mask over the head of the mummy,

Fig. 28. Pitch from Djehutymose's mummy, adhered to interior of coffin base.

29

30

31

35

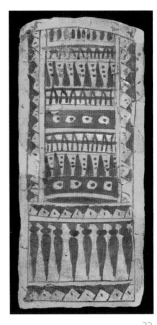

32

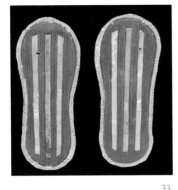

33

34

Fig. 29. Mummy mask, Ptolemaic Period, 332–30 BC, cloth, plaster, paint, gilding (KM 88778).

Fig. 30. Mummy mask, Ptolemaic Period, 332–30 BC, cloth, plaster, paint, gilding (KM 88776).

Fig. 31. Broad collar cartonnage, Late–Ptolemaic Periods, 525–30 BC, cloth, plaster, gilding (KM 88761).

Fig. 32. Cartonnage fragment, Late–Ptolemaic Periods, 525–30 BC, cloth, plaster, paint (KM 88575).

Fig. 33. Cartonnage sandal bottoms, Late–Ptolemaic Periods, 525–30 BC, cloth, plaster, paint, gilding (KM 88728).

Fig. 34. Cartonnage sandal bottoms, Late–Ptolemaic Periods, 525–30 BC, cloth, plaster, paint (KM 88729).

Fig. 35. Cartonnage foot covering, Late–Ptolemaic Periods, 525–30 BC, cloth, plaster, paint (KM 88581).

presenting an idealized image of Djehutymose similar to the head on the coffin (figs. 29–30), while other cartonnage pieces might be placed on the body and over the feet, covered with protective images and texts (figs. 31–35). Alternatively, Djehutymose's mummy may have been covered with a bead net, an elaborately decorated webbing of strung, colored beads. Bead nets often had texts and funerary images woven into their design, sometimes in imitation of the kinds of decoration on the coffin lid. Sometimes bead nets were placed on the mummy and then covered with cartonnage elements.[19] Once all such decorations were in place, the mummy was ready for burial.

Fig. 36. Scene from the Djehutymose coffin showing Anubis embalming Djehutymose.

Djehutymose's coffin itself contains a striking image of his embalming that sums up the divine precedent for this practice. In the very center of the coffin lid we see the jackal-headed god of embalming Anubis, holding an incense burner over a mummy on a lion-headed couch; beneath the couch sit four canopic jars, while above the scene hovers a *ba*-bird, the human-headed representation of the mobile, free-flying spiritual component of the dead man (fig. 36). On one level, this scene shows Djehutymose's own embalming: the mummy is Djehutymose's mummy, the canopic jars his, the *ba*-bird his own soul, and the Anubis figure a priest disguised as the god of embalming. On another level, however, this scene represents the first embalming, that of the god Osiris. In Egyptian mythology, Osiris was killed and dismembered by his jealous brother Seth. Osiris' wife Isis gathered the pieces of Osiris' body with the help of her sister Nephthys, and the pieces were wrapped together by Anubis (fig. 37) (sometimes described as the son of Nephthys) in linen bandages to form the first mummy. Thus prepared and magically revived by Isis, Osiris fathered his son Horus after death and went on to become the god of the dead. Osiris presided over the judgment of the dead accompanied by the four sons of Horus, whose heads are represented on the canopic jars, which are also inscribed with their names. These two readings of the same image are not an accident: by explicitly identifying Djehutymose's embalming with that of Osiris, the identification of the dead human with the regenerated god creates a parallel that will facilitate Djehutymose's own afterlife rebirth.[20]

This parallel with Osiris was important because preservation of the body was a crucial factor for Djehutymose's afterlife. Having a recognizable, preserved, intact body was a necessity: Djehutymose's spiritual components, especially his *ka* (variously characterized as the "double" and "life force" of the dead person) and *ba* (the mobile "personality" of the deceased),[21] needed a body to reside in or return to, and this body had to be identifiable as Djehutymose. Hence we have the reason for all of the effort to preserve and protect the body. The identification of the body as Djehutymose's is also reinforced by the frequent repetition of his name and titles on the coffin: all of these were further insurance that Djehutymose's *ba* and *ka* could recognize the body in the coffin as theirs. (The parents' names and titles ensured that this was the *right* Djehutymose, necessary given the popularity of this common name.) Indeed, the name itself was so important for identification that it was seen as yet another spiritual (or at

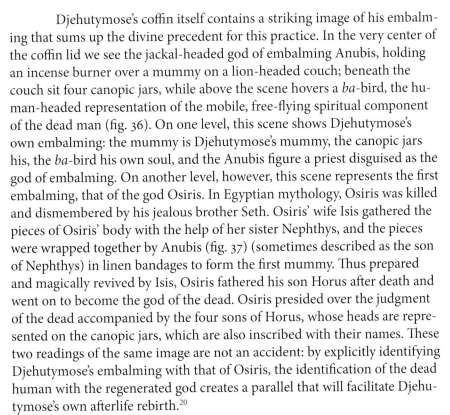

Fig. 37. Anubis amulet, Ptolemaic Period, 332–30 BC, bronze (KM 1971.2.141).

Fig. 38. Djehutymose's mummy as depicted in the embalming scene in fig. 36.

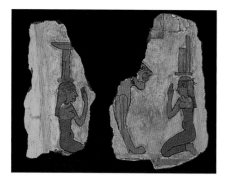

Fig. 39. Isis and Nephthys on cartonnage fragments, Late–Ptolemaic Periods, 525–30 BC, cloth, plaster, paint (KM 1981.4.31a–b).

least nonphysical) component of the dead person. As an important part of Djehutymose's identity, his name would have been written on any objects buried with him and inscribed on the decorations that covered his body.

Djehutymose's body, embalmed, wrapped, and decorated, was now ready for his funeral (fig. 38). Although not as lavish as those of earlier periods, elite funerals in the Saite Period were still occasions for display of wealth and importance. At a minimum, Djehutymose's coffin, mummy, and any other grave goods, along with offerings for the dead man, would have gone to his tomb in a procession accompanied by family members, friends, colleagues, officiating priests, and hired mourners. These mourners would have wailed in a ritual display of grief—their numbers and abilities were an indication of how many skilled professionals Djehutymose's family was able to hire and also a symbol of the extent of the family's grief. Their enacted mourning would also reinforce divine precedent, evoking the lamentations that Isis and her sister Nephthys made for the dead Osiris (fig. 39). The priests would read ritual texts, burn incense, and carry out other ceremonial duties. Once the procession had reached the tomb, the priests would perform the most important ritual of all on Djehutymose's mummy: the opening of the mouth. A designated priest would touch the mouth of the mummy (or, more precisely, the mummy's mask) with a special tool in a ritual designed to guarantee that the dead man could eat and drink his offerings. These actions also allowed him to breathe (in order to live) and speak after death. Given the endless interrogations Djehutymose would be subject to after death, all of which he would have to answer correctly, the opening of the mouth was crucial not only for life but also for survival and for transformation into an effective spirit.[22] Once his mouth was opened for eternity, Djehutymose's mummy would be placed in its coffin and put in the burial chamber of the tomb.

Although the precise location of Djehutymose's tomb is unknown, a text on the coffin refers specifically to his wish that he be buried in "the West of Edfu" (see below, page 84). "The West" is the ideal funerary direction and also the generic name for the location where burials were ideally made, in the rocky desert cliffs on the west bank of the Nile. Many priests of Horus of Edfu from Djehutymose's time and later were buried in a cemetery in the low desert near Edfu, now known as Nag el-Hassiya.[23] This was the standard burial area for the elite inhabitants of Edfu, and Djehutymose almost certainly would have been buried there in his family tomb, among the family tombs of his priestly colleagues. His coffin even bears a small representation of a tomb chapel (fig. 40), although this is a stock representation of a style of tomb no longer in use.

In addition to Djehutymose's mummy and coffin, his funeral was a time for the placement of other objects in the tomb. By the Saite Period, the amount of funerary equipment included in all but the highest elite burials had been pared down considerably from earlier times: tombs were no longer furnished like a combination of home and temple with many objects of daily life and much ritual equipment, as was common in the New Kingdom.[24] Centuries of experience had shown elite Egyptians that their tombs were likely to be robbed, regardless of the status of their owners or any precautions they might take. Pragmatically, the Egyptians chose to concentrate resources on the preparation and decoration of the mummy and its coffin, along with a fairly limited range of essential funerary equipment. The internal organs removed from the body in embalming may have been placed in individual canopic jars enclosed in a chest (although in this period the organs might also be wrapped in packets and placed in the body during the wrapping).[25] The representation of canopic jars in the embalming scene on Djehutymose's coffin gives an idea of what his jars might have looked like (fig. 41). The dead were often buried with a set of shabti figures, magical mummiform servant figures designed to do work in the afterlife. Sets of 365 shabtis, plus special overseer figures for this magical workforce, were not uncommon in elite, priestly burials of the time, often packed in jars or specially made boxes. (Although not from the Djehutymose burial, the Kelsey Museum has a number of fragmentary Saite shabti figures, in addition to many later examples; fig. 42) Funerary papyri containing texts and images from the Egyptian Book of the Dead and other compositions had apparently gone out of fashion sometime around 850 BC, but a substantially revised version of the Book of the Dead was compiled sometime around 700 BC. Papyri containing this "Saite Recension" of the Book of the Dead began to appear around 650 BC, although such papyri would not become common until rather later.[26] No Book of the Dead papyri are known to come from Saite burials at Edfu, and Djehutymose is unlikely to have had such a papyrus. Saite and later burials often include wooden or stone stelae—memorial tablets with funerary prayers and representations of the deceased; a number of stelae for Saite priests of Horus of Edfu are known to come from the Nag el-Hassiya cemetery, and Djehutymose may well have

Fig. 40. Representation of a tomb, from the foot of the coffin lid.

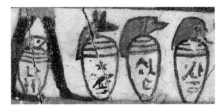

Fig. 41. Canopic jars inscribed with the names of the four sons of Horus, from the embalming scene in fig. 36.

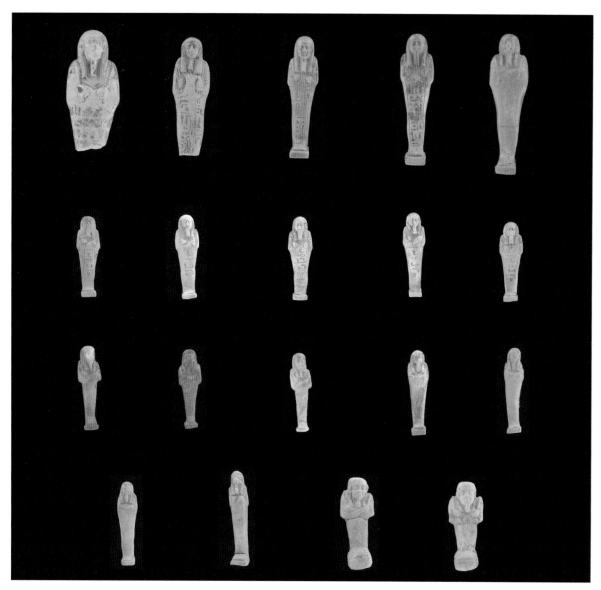

Fig. 42. Later shabti figures in the Kelsey Museum of Archaeology: *top row:* Saite–Late Period shabtis, c. 664–332 BC (*left to right:* KM 4648, 1980.4.33, 1971.2.162, 1971.2.151, 1981.5.35); *second row:* shabtis of Padihap from the Michigan Terenouthis excavation, Ptolemaic Period, 332–30 BC (*left to right:* KM 92257, 92254, 92263, 92261, 92262); *third and fourth rows:* anonymous shabtis from the Michigan Terenouthis excavation, Ptolemaic Period 332–30 BC (*third row, left to right:* KM 92248, 92250, 92247, 92556, 92342; *fourth row, left to right:* KM 92341, 92343, 92253, 92249).

43   44   45   46

had a stela of his own.[27] Pottery and other items, including divine figures of wood and personal items, might also be placed in the tomb. Finally, figures of a composite funerary god, Ptah-Sokar-Osiris, were often included in Saite elite burials. Placement of such objects in a tomb, especially in the case of a communal family tomb, would have depended on available space. In a Ptolemaic Period (332–30 BC) burial found intact at Nag el-Hassiya in 1905 by archaeologist John Garstang, the coffin was placed next to the tomb wall, while canopic chest, stela, and Ptah-Sokar-Osiris figure were grouped near the coffin's head.[28] Djehutymose may have been buried with a similar arrangement of objects.

Of these different kinds of funerary objects, we have a Ptah-Sokar-Osiris figure inscribed for Djehutymose (figs. 43–44), as well as a similar figure made for Djehutymose's brother (figs. 45–46) and and one

Fig. 43. Ptah-Sokar-Osiris figure of Djehutymose, front (on modern base), c. 625–580 BC, Nag el-Hassiya, wood, paint (KM 88768).

Fig. 44. Ptah-Sokar-Osiris figure of Djehutymose, back, c. 625–580 BC, Nag el-Hassiya, wood, paint (KM 88768).

Fig. 45. Ptah-Sokar-Osiris figure of Patjenefy (on modern base), front, c. 625–580 BC, Nag el-Hassiya, wood, paint, gilding (KM 88769).

Fig. 46. Ptah-Sokar-Osiris figure of Patjenefy (on modern base), back, c. 625–580 BC, Nag el-Hassiya, wood, paint, gilding (KM 88769).

Fig. 47. Ptah-Sokar-Osiris figure of Tareru? (on modern base), front, c. 625–580 BC or earlier, Nag el-Hassiya, wood, paint (KM 88770).

Fig. 48. Ptah-Sokar-Osiris figure of Tareru? (on modern base), back, c. 625–580 BC or earlier, Nag el-Hassiya, wood, paint (KM 88770).

Fig. 49. Ptah-Sokar-Osiris figures of Dje-hutymose, *left* (KM 88768) and his brother Patjenefy, *right* (KM 88769), showing relative size (on modern bases), c. 625–580 BC, Nag el-Hassiya, wood, paint, gilding.

47   48   49

that might belong to his mother (figs. 47–48), which strongly suggest that they were buried in the same tomb as Djehutymose. Each of these figures is made of wood covered with gesso and painted, and each represents a mummiform, bearded deity wearing a headdress of feathers, curvy horns, and solar disk common to representations of this composite god (Tareru's possible figure has lost its horns). Ptah-Sokar-Osiris combined three gods usually represented as mummies into a single figure, mingling the gods' respective attributes and powers as well as allowing a single image to represent all three. The form of the god in these figures most closely resembles traditional images of Osiris but can be distinguished by the headdress, different from Osiris' usual white crown. Both Djehutymose's and Patjenefy's figures are similar in style, with elaborate decoration on their bodies, and only the sizes and colors of the faces distinguish them: Djehutymose's own figure has a traditionally Osirian green face, like his coffin, while Patjenefy's larger figure has a face covered in gold (fig. 49). The larger size and gilded face of Patjenefy's figure may indicate his greater wealth, possibly a result of his additional priestly office. The figures' similar colors and styles suggest that they might have been made in the same workshop as Djehutymose's coffin. The figure that may belong to Tareru is damaged to the extent that the texts identifying the owner are not fully readable and the identification is uncertain; it is much more simply made and differs in many details from the other two. The brothers' figures bear standard inscriptions on front and back, including the common formula: "A royal offering of Osiris, Foremost of the Westerners," followed by the name and title of the dead person for whom it was made.[29]

These Ptah-Sokar-Osiris figures were symbols of afterlife regeneration and often included attributes to underline this purpose. The three figures have pegs under their feet clearly intended to slot into a base, which no longer survives. Parallels show that the bases of such figures in this period were usually rectangular, similarly made of wood and painted, often with inscriptions. Earlier types of Ptah-Sokar-Osiris figures contained papyri, either in the figure or in the base, but this was no longer a common practice in the Saite Period. Instead, Saite Ptah-Sokar-Osiris figures sometimes had an object known as a "grain mummy" concealed in the base.[30] A grain mummy is a figure in the shape of the god Osiris, made of mud containing grains of emmer or barley (the most common food grains in pharaonic Egypt), and sometimes wrapped as a mummy in cloth bandages and decorated. Grain mummies served as metaphors for the regeneration of the dead person in the afterlife: the grain inside the mummy would germinate and sprout, creating new life in a dead body. Some of these grain mummies are made in the form of the god Osiris, often represented with an erect penis to reinforce their metaphor of afterlife vitality and regeneration. Grain mummies could be quite elaborate, with their own coffins (often in the shape of the mummiform, falcon-headed funerary god Sokar) and decorated in the form of Osiris, as in an example in the Kelsey Museum that has a green wax Osiris face (fig. 50). Grain mummies of the sort stored in Ptah-Sokar-Osiris figure bases, however, tended to be smaller and less elaborately decorated; they were usually not in a separate coffin but covered in their cavity in the base by a lid surmounted by a falcon figure, probably in allusion to the falcon-headed god Sokar. Although neither bases nor grain mummies survive from Djehutymose's Ptah-Sokar-Osiris figures, two elaborately decorated wooden falcons that came to the museum with the figures may have served as coverings for the grain mummies in their bases (figs. 51–53).

Fig. 50. Grain mummy and coffin, Saite–Late Periods, 664–332 BC, wood, paint, mud, grain, cloth, pitch, wax (KM 88802).

Fig. 51. Falcon, possibly from base of Ptah-Sokar-Osiris figure of Djehutymose, c. 625–580 BC, Nag el-Hassiya, wood, paint (KM 88767).

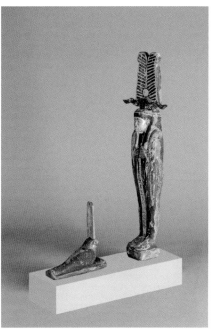

Fig. 53. Reconstruction of Ptah-Sokar-Osiris figure of Patjenefy (KM 88769) on base, showing possible placement of falcon (KM 88766) as cover for cavity with grain mummy.

Thus Djehutymose was brought to his tomb with his coffin and at least a Ptah-Sokar-Osiris figure, probably also accompanied by more objects, in his funeral procession. Rituals would have proceeded on the usual plan, but we know that Djehutymose's funeral did not go without a hitch. At some point, and it seems most likely that it was when the mummy was placed inside the coffin at the tomb, a terrible discovery was made: Djehutymose's mummy did not fit into his coffin! This is perhaps not as surprising as it might seem: the mummy and coffin were prepared separately. Also, elite mummies from the Saite Period tend to be heavily wrapped, even "puffy,"[31] and it must have been very hard to estimate the size of cavity needed for the body inside the coffin. However it happened, something urgently needed to be done to permit Djehutymose to be buried. Reduction of the mummy's bulk was not an option, so parts of the interior of the coffin had to be chipped away, at the shoulders and feet in both lid and base, so that the mummy could fit into the coffin (figs. 54–56). Such mishaps

Fig. 52. Falcon, possibly from base of Ptah-Sokar-Osiris figure of Patjenefy, c. 625–580 BC, Nag el-Hassiya, wood, paint, gilding (KM 88766).

were not uncommon in Egyptian burials and could plague even the most important individuals. The entombment of King Tutankhamun (the famous "King Tut") was halted by such an incident: the foot of his outer gold coffin projected just above the rim of his stone sarcophagus, causing the lid to crack when put into place. The foot of the coffin was hastily planed down (chips of wood were found beneath the coffin, showing that this was done in some haste) and the stone sarcophagus lid quickly and not very tidily patched and painted to cover the damage.[32] Djeuhtymose's problem was not quite so dramatic but must have been disruptive nonetheless: the fact that the damage inside the coffin (destroying part of the protective texts inside) was not in any way repaired suggests a similarly hasty action at the burial rather than an earlier mishap at the embalmers. After this act was carried out, Djehutymose was at last sealed in his coffin and placed in the tomb with his Ptah-Sokar-Osiris figure and his other funerary items, alongside the dead relatives already buried there. Once in his tomb, Djehutymose would rely on his coffin for both guidance and protection on his journey to the afterlife.

54

55

56

Fig. 54. Damage to coffin lid interior: portions removed to fit mummy.

Fig. 55. Figure of the goddess Nut on coffin lid interior, showing locations of damage.

Fig. 56. Damage to coffin lid interior: portions removed to fit mummy.

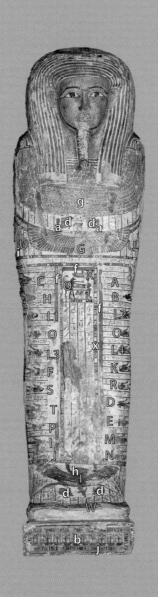

Diagram showing positions of gods and symbols on the Djehutymose coffin

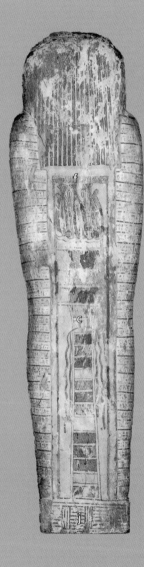

SYMBOLS
ⓐ Ankh
ⓑ Ankh-Was-Neb motif
ⓒ Djed pillar
ⓓ Eye of Horus
ⓔ Shen
ⓕ Sky
ⓖ Broad collar
ⓗ Nub
ⓘ Standard
ⓙ Borders

DJEHUTYMOSE'S GODS
A Re-Harakhte
B Khepri
C Atum
D Shu
E Tefnut
F Geb
G Nut
H Osiris
I Isis
J Nephthys
K Horus
L Four Sons of Horus:
 L1 Imsety
 L2 Hapy
 L3 Duamutef
 L4 Qebehsenuf
M Neith
N Serqet
O Anubis
P Wepwawet
Q Amentet
R Kherybakef
S Hekamaitef
T Iryrenefdjesef
U Banebdjedet
V Apis
W Mehen (snake)
X *Ba* bird

Djehutymose's Gods

While the basic form and face of the Djehutymose coffin represent the dead man as the god Osiris, the rest of the coffin is covered with the images and names of other gods and goddesses, all of whom played a role in Djehutymose's transformation from dead man to effective spirit in the afterlife. The protective function of Djehutymose's gods can be seen in their positioning: winged goddesses spread their protective wings over his head, chest, and feet, while other protective goddesses spread their arms around his body on the interior of his coffin. A procession of protective deities lines the flanks of both sides of Djehutymose's coffin, and a protective snake encircles the entirety of the coffin lid. From the top of its head, capped by an image of the goddess Nephthys, to the bottom of its feet, with an image of the Apis bull, the coffin of Djehutymose is covered, inside and out, head to toe, with divine images invoking the protection of a wide range of deities.

Egyptian gods and goddesses are represented in very specific ways, bound by the conventions of Egyptian art and the Egyptian concept of decorum, which determined what could and could not be represented or mentioned, as well as the Egyptians' understandings of their deities' appearances. Proportions and style of representation are formal, set, and relatively rigid. The gods, in general, are shown as youthful, vigorous beings but dressed in very conservative fashion: the kilts with tails for male gods and the long, strapped sheath dresses for female goddesses represent archaic styles from a very early period in Egyptian history. The gods' costumes almost serve as a uniform to emphasize their antiquity and also set them apart from humans. As if to make up for the relative simplicity of their attire, the gods show great variety in their headdresses and other attributes. Many gods have standard, set attributes that allowed even a nonliterate person to determine the identity of a god in an image. Many are closely identified with specific animals and often appear in human form but with the heads of their associated animal or entirely in animal form. The gods' skin color in representations is often symbolic: the frequency of gods with green or blue skin on the Djehutymose coffin, for example, emphasizes rebirth and regeneration.

The Egyptian gods all have individual names and identities, but their roles and interrelationships are complicated by the fact that Egyptian religion developed out of many different local traditions, brought together in late prehistory as Egypt was coalescing as a political and cultural entity. The result is a set of mythologies that sometimes appear contradictory: Egyptian religion accommodated many different creation traditions, for example, while the god Horus can be described variously as the son or brother of the goddess Isis but also as the son, husband, or father of the goddess Hathor. These apparent contradictions were not, as far as we can tell, a problem for the ancient Egyptians. Gods could merge, and often did, sometimes for political reasons: thus, the relatively obscure Theban god Amun was merged, when Thebes became an important center of power, with the major sun-god Re to become "Amun-Re, king of the gods." Individual gods can also have many different forms or sub-identities: thus the god Horus has such forms as Horus-the-Child (Harpocrates), Horus-son-of-Isis (Harseise), Horus-the-Elder, Horakhte, Horus-of-Edfu, and, on the Djehutymose coffin, Horus-without-eyes-in-his-forehead. Each of these is "Horus," but they are also distinctive beings in their own right.[33]

Solar gods were of great importance in Egyptian religion. Seen as the oldest, ancestral gods in the Egyptian pantheon, they were among the most senior and most powerful, appropriate in an arid land that received so much sunlight. In the Egyptian understanding of the world, the sun went around the earth and was often represented doing so in a boat. The sun-god's daytime journey through the sky was mirrored by a mysterious night-time journey through the Netherworld. The solar gods were worshipped at temples throughout Egypt, but one of the oldest and most important centers was at Heliopolis (north of modern Cairo), where Djehutymose's father had a priestly appointment. Three solar gods appear on Djehutymose's coffin in the processions on Djehutymose's flanks.

The representation of **Re-Harakhte** at the head of the procession on Djehutymose's left side is badly damaged, but enough survives to show the god had a falcon head and wore a sun-disk surrounded by a serpent (fig. 57). The attributes of Re-Harakhte are easier to see in a Third Intermediate Period funerary papyrus in the University of Michigan Library Papyrology Collection (fig. 58). Re-Harakhte is, in fact, a combination of the ancient sun-god Re with the possibly even older god Horus (in his form of Horus-of-the-horizon) to be the god of the midday sun.

Directly following Re-Harakhte in the left-side procession of gods is **Khepri**, the god of the morning sun when it rises in the east. Represented in human form, Khepri wears on his head the scarab beetle that is his

Fig. 57. Damaged representation of the god Re-Harakhte from the Djehutymose coffin.

Fig. 58. Image of Re-Harakhte, Book of the Dead papyrus of Djed-Mut, 21st–22nd Dynasty, c. 1000–800 BC, papyrus, ink, paint (P. Mich. inv. 3524, University of Michigan Library Papyrology Collection).

Fig. 59. The god Khepri.

Fig. 60. Scarab applique, Ptolemaic Period, 332–30 BC, faience (KM 1983.1.60).

Fig. 61. Scarab, , Ptolemaic–Early Roman Periods, 332 BC–AD 100, faience (KM 24189).

Fig. 62. The god Atum.

Glyph 2. Scarab hieroglyph.

symbol—hieroglyph for his name as well as the Egyptian word "to come into being" (fig. 59, glyph 2). The symbol is significant for this god of the morning sun. The scarab beetle lays its eggs in a ball of dung that it rolls around. The eventual hatching of eggs from an apparently inert ball of matter is a potent metaphor for the sun's life-giving properties, and Khepri is often represented as a beetle rolling the disk of the sun through the sky. The scarab was one of the most common amulets in ancient Egypt and can be seen in many examples in the Kelsey Museum (figs. 60–61).

Heading the procession of gods on the other side of Djehutymose's coffin is the sun-god **Atum** (fig. 62). Dressed as a king wearing the double crown of Upper and Lower Egypt, Atum is represented as entirely human, although often elsewhere shown as having a ram's head. Atum is closely associated with creation, as a god who created himself out of the watery nothingness known as Nun. Atum is the god of the setting sun and, as such, the form of the sun that goes into the Netherworld in the sun's nighttime journey, which is described in such texts as the Book of Amduat.

63

64

65

In one of the major Egyptian creation stories, the Heliopolitan cosmology, the sun-god Atum creates himself and then creates two children, the god **Shu** and the goddess **Tefnut** (fig. 63). Shu and Tefnut are associated with dry air and moisture respectively in their roles as early elemental gods. They appear on this coffin in the divine procession, but their figures are badly damaged. It is possible to see the feather atop Shu's head (a common attribute of the god), but the damage makes it impossible to tell if Tefnut is represented with a lion head, as is common—it looks as if she has a human head, topped by a feather like Shu's. Shu is often shown holding up the sky, as in an amulet in the Kelsey Museum (fig. 64).

Shu and Tefnut ultimately became the parents of the god **Geb** and the goddess Nut, associated with the earth and the sky, respectively, in the Heliopolitan cosmology, where the early generations of gods bring about the major elements and institutions. Geb is represented in the procession of the gods in human form, albeit very heavily damaged (fig. 65). In addition to his speech in connection with this representation, Geb appears repeatedly as a speaker in texts elsewhere on the coffin, where he is identified by his title "hereditary prince of the gods."

Fig. 63. The god Shu (*right*) and goddess Tefnut (*left*).

Fig. 64. Shu amulet, Late–Ptolemaic Periods, 525–30 BC, faience (KM 1971.2.58).

Fig. 65. The god Geb.

Fig. 66. The goddess Nut, represented with wings, from the chest of the coffin.

Fig. 67. The goddess Nut, as depicted in the interior of the coffin lid.

Nut is not part of either procession, but she appears much more prominently elsewhere on the Djehutymose coffin. She is depicted, in winged form, below Djehutymose's head, her wings spread across Djehutymose's chest in a gesture of protection (goddesses are often shown with wings when they serve protective functions, as we see elsewhere on the coffin) (fig. 66). This winged Nut wears a sun-disk on her head that has the hieroglyphs for her name inside; she also wears a headband with a sacred cobra in front.

More dramatically, Nut appears in an unusual full-frontal image on the inside of the coffin lid, in the guise of her role as sky goddess acting as a literal sky (fig. 67). She is stretched out, arms raised and hair falling down over her head, standing on tiptoes, wearing a blue dress covered in stars: in this guise Nut *is* the sky, her body stretched over the earth. During the day, the sun travels over her body. At night, in some traditions, Nut swallows the sun and it travels through her body, coming out at dawn when she gives birth to it. Two sun-disks on this representation inside Djehutymose's coffin show the sun just prior to being swallowed by Nut at dusk and just after she gives birth to it at dawn (a third is beneath her feet, enclosed in a shen sign).[34]

In some traditions, Nut gives birth to five children, fathered by Geb (in some versions, Shu separates Geb and Nut while they are having sex, thus creating the division between earth and sky). Nut's five children are born on the five "extra" (or, more precisely, "epagomenal") days at the end of the 365-day Egyptian calendar (after 12 regular months of 30 days), and these children become important gods in the Egyptian pantheon: Osiris, Isis, Nephthys, Seth, and, in some versions of the story, a form of the god Horus.

Fig. 68. Grain mummy, Saite–Late Periods, 664–332 BC, mud, grain, cloth, pitch, wax (KM 88802).

Fig. 69. Votive figures of the god Osiris, Late–Ptolemaic Periods, 525–30 BC, bronze (KM 3146, 21601–21606, 21610–21212, 21614, 1971.2.140).

Fig. 70. The god Osiris.

68   69

70

Osiris appears implicitly in the overall form of Djehutymose's coffin and is invoked in every mention of Djehutymose in the texts, where he is constantly identifed as "Osiris Djehutymose"—that is to say, "the late Djehutymose." The implication is specifically that Djehutymose has become like Osiris and is reborn in the afterlife. Osiris is usually depicted as a mummy with a green face and beard, wearing the White Crown of an Egyptian king (often with additional feathers on the side). In this guise he is seen in a number of later period Egyptian objects in the Kelsey Museum collection, most notably the grain mummy discussed above and a large number of bronze figures left as votive offerings at temples (figs. 68–69). Rather less typically, Osiris is shown on the Djehutymose coffin in the procession of gods on the right flank as a striding figure, not a mummy, but with his usual green skin, beard, and crown (fig. 70). Osiris' kingly attributes are due to his role as (legendary) first king of Egypt. He is sometimes identified as Osiris Wennefer, or simply **Wennefer**, a title or attribute referring to his goodness. Otherwise, he is also identified by the title "Foremost of the Westerners," which is actually the name of the very ancient funerary god Khentiamentiu that becomes a title relating to Osiris' primacy in the funerary region of the West.

Isis was not only Osiris' sister but was also his wife, and she participated as his queen in his royal role. But Isis was a goddess with a considerable independent identity of her own. She was widely known as a goddess of magic, who could even trick the powerful sun-god Re, and also as a special protector of mothers and children, thanks to her own adventures in connection with the birth and childhood of her son Horus. Isis appears

Fig. 71. The goddess Isis, represented with wings, from the foot of the coffin lid.

Fig. 72. The goddesses Isis (*left*) and Nephthys (*right*).

Fig. 73. The goddess Nephthys, represented with wings, from the head of the coffin lid.

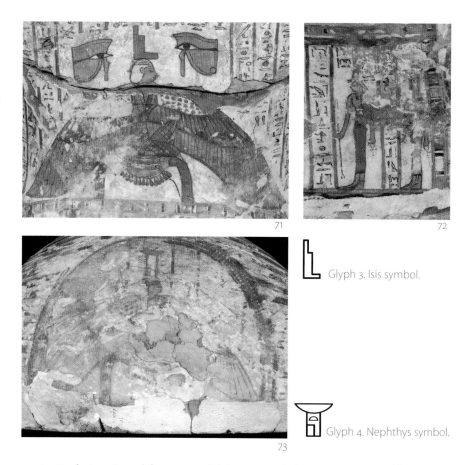

Glyph 3. Isis symbol.

Glyph 4. Nephthys symbol.

protectively in winged form over Djehutymose's feet, accompanied by a magical spell (fig. 71), and she also appears in the divine procession (fig. 72). She can be identified by the special headdress she often wears, a symbol of a throne (glyph 3).

Isis is followed in the procession by her sister **Nephthys**. Although this image is badly damaged, one can see her wearing her characteristic headdress consisting of a palace and basket (glyph 4). A winged representation of Nephthys appears protectively on the top of Djehutymose's head—even more damaged although it is possible in this image to see Nephthys' head as well as her headdress and wings (fig. 73). Nephthys is known primarily for her association with Isis but also as the wife of her brother **Seth**. Seth was a trickster god and agent of chaos, so it is not surprising

Fig. 74. A Horus falcon, from Djehutymose's broad collar.

Fig. 75. The god Horus in his form Horus-without-eyes-in-his-forehead.

that he does not appear on the Djehutymose coffin. In the classic legend, Seth killed his brother Osiris in order to take the throne of Egypt and then fought Osiris' proper successor, his son Horus. Although a transgressive figure in many ways, Seth served a major role in Egyptian mythology and, in spite of his misdeeds, was a god of considerable seniority and importance.

Nut's fifth child was, in some versions of the myth, known as **Horus**, a god whose place in the Egyptian mythological family tree is seemingly contradictory. Horus was a god from very early in Egyptian history and had to be accommodated into a variety of mythological traditions, often in different forms. Thus, he was, in some form, a son of Nut and Geb, but was primarily known as the son of Isis and Osiris (one tradition deals with this issue most ingeniously by describing him as a son of Isis and Osiris conceived while they were still in Nut's womb!).[35] Horus' most ancient associations are solar and royal, and because he ultimately succeeded to Osiris' kingship, his story reflects the paradigm of the ideal of royal succession from king to eldest son. Horus is often represented as a falcon or as a human with a falcon head, and he appears in both guises on the Djehutymose coffin. The falcon head terminals of the broad collar around Djehutymose's neck allude generically to Horus (fig. 74). A more specialized form of Horus is shown by one of the falcon-headed figures in the divine procession Horus-without-eyes-in-his-forehead (fig. 75).[36] Horus' eyes are important symbols in their own right, as we will see below. Other images of

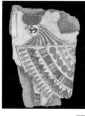

76   77

Fig. 76. Falcon amulet, Late–Ptolemaic Periods, 525–30 BC, faience (KM 1971.2.62).

Fig. 77. Falcon head on cartonnage fragment, Late–Ptolemaic Periods, 525–30 BC, cloth, plaster, paint (KM 1981.4.32).

Fig. 78. The four sons of Horus: Imsety.

Fig. 79. The four sons of Horus: Hapy.

Fig. 80. The four sons of Horus: Duamutef.

Fig. 81. The four sons of Horus: Qebehsenuf.

Horus in the Kelsey Museum include a faience falcon figure and a piece of cartonnage showing a falcon head (figs. 76–77).

The gods often travel and associate in groups, and the foregoing gods often came together in a group of nine gods known as the **Ennead**, occasionally referred to as such in the texts on Djehutymose's coffin. The makeup of the Ennead varies, but the references in Djehutymose's coffin probably refer to a standard Ennead made up of the earliest generations of the gods—typically a sun-god (Re, Atum, Khepri, or some related god), followed by Shu and Tefnut, Geb and Nut, Osiris and Isis, Nephthys and Seth or Horus. The Ennead is often represented as traveling in a solar boat with the sun-god at the head.

Horus himself has four sons, one of whom is the other falcon-headed figure in the divine procession. Indeed all of Horus' four sons appear in the processions and can be distinguished by their heads: **Imsety** (human-headed, fig. 78), **Hapy** (baboon-headed, fig. 79), **Duamutef** (jackal-headed, fig. 80), and **Qebehsenuf** (falcon-headed, fig. 81). Although

78   79   80   81

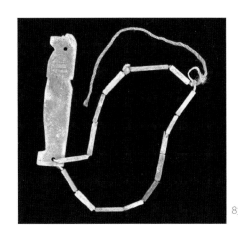

shown as freely striding figures in the procession, the four sons of Horus are more often shown as mummies, as in these Kelsey Museum amulets (figs. 82–83). The four sons of Horus are associated with the four directions (North, South, East, West) and the four canopic jars that contain the internal organs of the deceased, jars frequently represented with the respective heads of their gods, as in the embalming scene on the Djehutymose coffin (see fig. 41 above).

Isis and Nephthys are also deities associated with canopic jars, along with the goddesses **Neith** and **Serqet** (or **Selqet**), both of whom are shown in the divine procession (fig. 84). Although the figures of both goddesses are damaged, their attributes are visible. Neith is a very ancient goddess, sometimes associated with war, and she wears the Red Crown of Lower Egypt. Serqet (or Selqet: *r* and *l* are not distinguished in earlier Egyptian) wears a scorpion on her head, an attribute symbolic of her powers against scorpions and other dangerous animals.

The jackal-headed god **Anubis** is sometimes described as the son of Nephthys and Seth (or even Nephthys and Osiris). He is a god most often associated with embalming and, in particular, his role as embalmer of the dead Osiris and thus creator of the first mummy. Wild dogs, and particularly jackals, are scavengers, and their association of this god with embalming may have initially come about from seeing them digging up human remains. Anubis appears twice in the divine procession, once as Anubis Who Is in

Fig. 82. Duamutef amulet, Late–Ptolemaic Periods, 525–30 BC, faience (KM 1980.4.40).

Fig. 83. Hapi amulet, Late–Ptolemaic Periods, 525–30 BC, faience (KM 1980.4.41).

Fig. 84. The goddesses Neith (*right*) and Serqet (*left*).

Fig. 85. The god Anubis, Who Is in the Place of Embalming

Fig. 86. The god Anubis, Foremost of the Divine Booth.

Fig. 87. The god Anubis, from the embalming scene in fig. 36.

Fig. 88. Anubis jackal (on modern base), Saite–Late Periods, 664–332 BC, wood, paint (KM 1971.2.185).

Fig. 89. The god Wepwawet.

the Place of Embalming (fig. 85) and once as Anubis Foremost of the Divine Booth (fig. 86), probably also an allusion to the embalming chamber. Anubis further appears in the scene showing the embalming of a mummy, described above (fig. 87). Images of Anubis are frequently found in Egyptian funerary art, as a jackal-headed human or as a jackal, as in a Kelsey Museum wooden tomb statue and a bronze amulet (fig. 88 and fig. 37 above).

Frequently associated with Anubis is another nearly identical jackal- or dog-headed god, **Wepwawet** (fig. 89). His name means, literally, "Opener of the Ways," and Wepwawet serves funerary functions as well by opening paths for the dead person in the Netherworld. He appears just following Anubis in the divine procession, and representations of the two gods together are common, as in this image from a coffin in the Kelsey Museum (fig. 90).

Another specifically funerary deity can be seen in the large-scale image of the goddess **Amentet** on the interior of the coffin base (fig. 91).

90

91

Amentet is the goddess of the West—not just the cardinal direction but also the "West" as the ideal location for burial, the direction of the setting sun, and the point of access to the Netherworld. Amentet's name is also the Egyptian word for "West," and she is its personification. Amentet presides over cemeteries and burial sites, and her protection is crucial for the afterlife. Amentet wears on her head the falcon standard that is the hieroglyph for her name, and she stands on a standard herself. She wears an elaborately beaded dress, an intricately braided wig, and a red hair ribbon. Flowing red strips of cloth are tied to her arms, most likely allusions to red bandages used in mummification. She is dressed in a festive way that might seem, to a modern viewer, contradictory for a funerary goddess. But Egyptian funerals were, at heart, celebrations of the deceased, their status, and their afterlife, often accompanied by festive parties, so Amentet's costume is entirely appropriate for a celebration of eternal life. The figure of Amentet is positioned so that, when the mummy of Djehutymose was placed in the coffin base, Amentet's raised arms curve slightly around the mummy. Essentially, Amentet is embracing Djehutymose from behind: she has his back, in protective terms, and shelters him in her embrace.

Three relatively obscure gods are represented in the procession of gods on the coffin.[37] **Kherybakef** (literally, "he-who-is-under-his-moringa-

Fig. 90. Fragment of coffin showing Anubis and Wepwawet as jackals, Late–Ptolemaic Periods, 525–30 BC, wood, paint (KM 88725).

Fig. 91. The goddess Amentet.

Fig. 92. The god
Kherybakef.

Fig. 93. The god
Hekamaitef.

Fig. 94. The god
Iryrenefdjesef.

92 93 94

tree," fig. 92) was a very ancient Memphite tree god who was ultimately
absorbed into the major creator-god **Ptah** of Memphis (himself, in turn,
one component of the compound god Ptah-Sokar-Osiris). Kherybakef is
shown here with an ibis head. **Hekamaitef** is a protector of Osiris, and by
extension the dead Djehutymose (his name means, literally, "Prince-who-
sees-his-father," fig. 93), and is represented in human form. Also shown
in human form is the god **Iryrenefdjesef**, whose name means "He-who-
made-his-name-himself" (fig. 94). These gods often appear on the flanks of
coffins of this period.

Other gods appear on the Djehutymose coffin in their animal
forms alone. On either side of the winged Nut figure over Djehutymose's
chest are images of the ram-god **Banebdjedet** (fig. 95). In both instances
the images are damaged, but one can see that the ram is standing on an
archaic standard behind an image of the hieroglyph that begins his name
(glyph 5). Banebdjedet was the ram god of Mendes, associated with sex-
ual power and vigor, who became a significant funerary god in the later

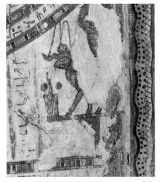

Glyph 5.
Ba sign.

95

96

97

periods. The ram is also a way of writing the word *ba*, "spirit," and this is found in some of the texts on the Djehutymose coffin. So these rams on the coffin may also be invoking more generally this usage as well.

On the foot of the coffin lid, the bull-god **Apis** appears, walking toward a tomb in a hillside, with an offering stand before him, wearing a solar disk on his head (fig. 96). The Apis bull cult is one of the oldest known animal cults from ancient Egypt, and Apis remained an important god throughout Egyptian history, often associated with Osiris. Coffins of later periods sometimes showed the mummy of the deceased being carried on the back of an Apis bull, so Apis was involved in the journey the deceased was taking, carrying the dead person to the afterlife. Apis is often represented in bronze figures like this example in the Kelsey Museum (fig. 97).

Finally, a snake figure that circles the lid of the Djehutymose coffin may well represent the snake god **Mehen**, a Netherworld god who protects the sun-god from his foes during his nighttime voyage and, by extension, protects Djehutymose as well. Snakes were ambiguous entities in Egyptian thought: poisonous snakes were a dangerous part of the living environment of Egyptians, and snakes often appear in adversarial relationships to the gods, the best known of these being the enemy of the sun-god known as Apophis. But snakes were also associated with protection, divinity, and kingship: kings and divinities wear cobras on the brows of their crowns and headdresses (fig. 98), and snakes were even mummified and buried as parts of animal cults. So snake gods like Mehen and Neheb-Ka (represented in an amulet in the Kelsey Museum—fig. 99) were protective and beneficent gods. Encircling was an act of magical protection[38] and an activity that snakes were uniquely equipped to carry out thanks to their anatomy. On

Fig. 95. The ram god Banebdjedet.

Fig. 96. The bull god Apis in scene on coffin foot in fig. 141.

Fig. 97. Apis bull figure, Late–Ptolemaic Periods, 525–30 BC, bronze (KM 1971.2.147).

Fig. 98. Cobra from the headdress of the goddess Nut, fig. 66.

Fig. 99. Amulet of the snake god Neheb-Ka, Ptolemaic Period, 332–30 BC, faience (KM 4633).

98

99

Fig. 100. Encircling snake, visible along lower edge of coffin lid.

Fig. 101. Snake circling around coffin lid foot.

Fig. 102. Head and tail of snake on coffin foot.

Fig. 103. *Ba* bird from scene on coffin lid foot in fig. 141.

Fig. 104. *Ba* bird hovering over mummy of Djehutymose in embalming scene in fig. 36.

100

102

101

103

104

the Djehutymose coffin, the snake encloses the lid image of Djehutymose completely (fig. 100), and the artist has paid careful attention to the representation of the dark scales on the snake's back and the lighter scales on its belly, the details being, rather unusually, not entirely delineated with black outlines but also picked out in colors (fig. 101). The artist has given even more attention to the representation of the snake's head meeting its tail just above the foot of the coffin: again, an unusual use of color gives the snake's head a particularly vivid expression (fig. 102).

One animal-human hybrid that appears twice on the coffin is not a god but rather a manifestation of a spiritual aspect of Djehutymose himself, the ***ba***. Represented as a bird with a human head, the *ba* is the mobile spiritual component of a dead person—the part that leaves the body at death and travels around. Images in the Egyptian Book of the Dead show the *ba* entering and leaving the tomb, and its mobility is emphasized when it is represented. The *ba* of Djehutymose appears twice on the coffin, once flying above the Apis bull on the foot of the coffin (fig. 103) and again hovering over the scene of embalming in the center of the lid (fig. 104). In this latter representation, the *ba*'s identity with Djehutymose is emphasized: the *ba*-bird is directly above the mummy, and the caption to the right, "Priest of Horus, Priest of the Golden One, Djehutymose," identifies both the mummy being embalmed and the *ba*-bird. They are both integral parts of Djehutymose.

A few important gods do not appear in images on the coffin but are still significant for it nonetheless. Thanks to his role in Djehutymose's name, the ibis that represents the god **Thoth** (Djehuty)[39] is inscribed all over the coffin, but he also plays a more active role in its texts (fig. 105). Thoth was an ancient and senior god in the Egyptian pantheon, frequently represented in human form with an ibis head (fig. 106). Thoth was the god of writing and the scribe of the gods, their record-keeper and messenger, arbitrator of their frequent disputes. For Djehutymose, the god Thoth would have acted almost as a legal representative in his final judgment; Thoth stands by the weighing of the heart, recording the verdict and delivering it to the judging gods. But Thoth also appears more directly in the texts of Djehutymose's coffin: he is the first speaker in the important text Book of the Dead, chapter 1, which is repeated twice on the coffin. Thoth acts on behalf of Osiris in this text and, by extension, on behalf of Djehutymose as well.

The funerary god **Sokar** appears only obliquely in Djehutymose's burial. Sokar is often represented as a human mummy with a falcon head (as in the coffin of the Kelsey Museum grain mummy—fig. 107). By the Saite Period he has more or less been subordinated to Osiris as primary god of the dead, but his ancient symbols are still important parts of funereal mythology in Egypt. Indeed, Sokar is often united with Osiris in the hybrid god Ptah-Sokar-Osiris, who plays an important role in Djehutymose's funerary equipment, as we have seen. Another ancient funerary god, **Khentiamentiu**, has essentially been absorbed into Osiris in the coffin of Djehutymose, his name being taken as a title of Osiris in its literal meaning of "Foremost of the Westerners," first of the gods in the funerary direction of the west. In his earlier, independent existence, Khentiamentiu was a jackal-headed god like Anubis and Wepwawet, associated with Abydos; the identity and functions of this very ancient god were ultimately taken over by Osiris, with whom be became identified.

105   106

107

Fig. 105. Image of the god Thoth as an ibis, used as a hieroglyph in Djehutymose's name.

Fig. 106. Thoth amulet, Late–Ptolemaic Periods, 525–30 BC, faience (KM 1971.2.85).

Fig. 107. Grain mummy coffin in the form of the god Sokar, Saite–Late Periods, 664–332 BC, wood, paint (KM 88802).

108   Glyph 6

109   Glyph 7

110   111   Glyph 8

112

Fig. 108. The goddess Nut holding ankh symbols, flanked by Eye of Horus symbols, fig. 66.

Fig. 109. The *ankh-was-neb* motif from the coffin lid foot.

Fig. 110. Djed pillar amulet, Ptolemaic Period, 332–30 BC, Terenouthis, Egypt, carnelian (KM 24201).

Fig. 111. Djed pillar amulet, Ptolemaic Period, 332–30 BC, Terenouthis, Egypt, faience (KM 24204).

Fig. 112. Djed pillar, with streamers, from coffin base exterior.

Djehutymose's Symbols

In addition to the images and names of gods, the Djehutymose coffin also bears a number of protective or magical symbols, often symbols that have linguistic significance as hieroglyphs as well. The meaning of these symbols goes well beyond what they ostensibly represent: they have gone on from relatively mundane origins to become potent signs of power and protection, deployed in a variety of ways to assist Djehutymose in his quest for an afterlife.

The **ankh** (glyph 6) represents the strap of a sandal but has the meaning of "life" and is a potent symbol in Egyptian thought. It appears very frequently in Egyptian art and is often worn, as are many of these symbols, as an amulet. Each of the 22 gods in the divine processions along the sides of the coffin carries an ankh symbol (some are now effaced), and the goddess Nut on the chest of the coffin carries two ankh symbols (fig. 108).

The ankh is incorporated into a decorative motif around the edge of the foot of the coffin, the **ankh-was-neb** (glyph 7) motif. An ankh sign is flanked by *was*-scepters on either side, sitting atop the *neb* sign (fig. 109). Groups of hieroglyphs used for decorative purposes like this also often have meaning and sometimes encode rebuses or brief sentences. Thinking in this way, we have the sign of "life" flanked by two signs usually translated as "dominion," all above a sign that can be read either "lord" or "all," and a literal rendering of this group might be "all life and dominion." Originally, Djehutymose's coffin had 36 of these groups around the front and sides of the foot, but a few have now been lost through damage.

The **Djed** pillar (glyph 8) came to represent the backbone of Osiris and is often translated as "stability." The Djed pillar is frequently placed as an amulet on mummies, and the Kelsey Museum collection includes a number of examples (figs. 110–111). Djed pillars also appear on coffins, and Djehutymose's coffin features an enormous example, covering most of the outside of the base of the coffin. Djehutymose's Djed pillar is decorated in blue, red, and green, adorned with red bandages (like the image of the goddess Amentet on the inside of the base), and topped with an elaborate triple atef crown, a crown often worn by Osiris (fig. 112). Indeed, the Djed pillar often serves as a stand-in for an image of Osiris or features in images of Osiris merged with a Djed pillar. So, in addition to its streamers mirroring those of Amentet on the other side of the base, this decorated Djed pillar

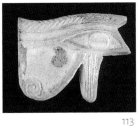

113   114   115   Glyph 9

also mirrors the Osirian lid of the coffin. Djed pillars are associated with the backs and necks of mummies, providing stability and strength, so the presence of this one on the back of the coffin is appropriate.

The **Eye of Horus** (glyph 9) represents the eye of the god Horus plucked out in a battle with Seth and regenerated by Thoth. It was a potent protective symbol, widely used as an amulet, as the many examples in a variety of materials preserved in the Kelsey Museum can attest (fig. 113). The Eye of Horus may have had special powers against the evil eye or eye disease (quite common in ancient Egypt) but was much more commonly used for general protective purposes and can also symbolize offerings.[40] The Eye of Horus often appears in pairs, and we see two pairs on the Djehutymose coffin: with the goddess Nut on the chest of the coffin and with the goddess Isis on the feet (figs. 114–115). Box-style coffins from earlier periods often feature pairs of Horus Eyes in an appropriate place to serve as windows for the deceased to see out of the coffin. This was not necessary with anthropoid coffins like Djehutymose's, which has eyes in the idealized image of the deceased, although later anthropoid coffins still sometimes include these eyes on the side.[41]

The **Shen** sign (glyph 10) is a symbol of eternity, representing a tied-off circle of rope, so its placement on Djehutymose's coffin is appropriate as representing the eternal nature of Djehutymose's hoped-for afterlife. Egyptian understandings of time were, in part, cyclical: time moved in eternal cycles and loops, and the shen sign encapsulates this way of seeing the progression of time. The goddess Nut stands on a shen sign (fig. 116), and the *ba* bird on the foot of the coffin holds one in its claws (fig. 117). Circles, especially circles that can enclose things, are potent magical symbols as well; indeed, the cartouche used to enclose kings' names in Egyptian writing is simply an elongated shen sign. It is significant that contemporary artist John Kannenberg was inspired by the image on Djehutymose's coffin to

Fig. 113. Eye of Horus amulet, Late–Ptolemaic Periods, 525–30 BC, faience (KM 1971.2.30).

Fig. 114. Eye of Horus from coffin lid foot.

Fig. 115. Eye of Horus from coffin lid foot.

Fig. 116. Shen symbol from beneath the feet of the goddess Nut, coffin lid interior.

Fig. 117. Shen symbol held by *ba* bird on coffin lid foot scene in fig. 141.

116

117

Glyph 10

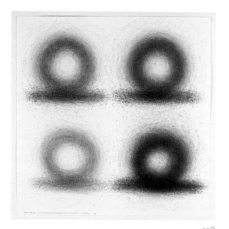

Glyph 11

119

120

121

Glyph 12

118

choose shen signs as one of the symbols of infinity for his Kelsey Museum exhibition and performance "Hours of Infinity" (fig. 118).[42]

The **sky** sign (glyph 11), sometimes covered in stars, is a hieroglyphic determinative for words that involve the sky or things that are high or above other things. Elongated and expanded, the sky sign can serve as a visual shorthand for events that take place outdoors, under or in the sky, as in the scene with the Apis bull on the foot of Djehutymose's coffin (fig. 119). The blue sky sign bears stars and sits above the scene in which the Apis bull approaches a mountainous cliff with a tomb set in it: the scene is outdoors but also set in eternity in the afterlife, the location of which is in the sky. Another sky sign, this one without stars, can be seen above the embalming scene on the chest of the lid, and very elongated sky signs top the processions of gods on either side of the coffin lid. Further, the thicker blue rectangle on the back of the coffin above the Djed pillar may also be a sky sign without stars (the damage to this area makes the artist's intent slightly unclear).

The broad **collar** (glyph 12) is not exclusively a symbol, and on the Djehutymose coffin it can be seen primarily as a representation of something that the late Djehutymose would have worn: a multi-rowed, floral collar, or more likely a bead collar in imitation of a floral collar, made with rows of faience or glass beads strung to terminal pieces in the shape of Horus heads and fastened at the back (fig. 120). These collars are ubiquitous in Egyptian art: humans and gods wear them in a variety of contexts, festive and funereal. But they also serve as symbols—used as hieroglyphs determining names for the broad collar but also as amulets, which become increasingly common in the Saite Period and later.[43] Compare this delicate gold collar amulet, probably Ptolemaic Period, from the Michigan excavations at Terenouthis (fig. 121).

The goddesses Nephthys (at Djehutymose's head) and Isis (at Djehutymose's feet) both kneel on **Nub** signs (glyph 13), the Egyptian hieroglyph for "gold" representing an elaborate necklace (fig. 122). The goddesses often traditionally sit on these signs for gold, especially on coffins, and other gods sit on them as well. In a funerary context, the gold sign may invoke the permanence and stability of gold as well as its value: the goddesses endure like gold and are also precious like the metal.[44]

Standard signs (glyph 14) represent the very ancient standards used to raise totemic images of animals and other symbols of early Egyptian gods. On the Djehutymose coffin, the two rams representing the god Banebdjedef are on standards, as is the goddess Amentet, who bears a falcon on a standard as her headdress (fig. 123). Indeed, by Djehutymose's time, the standard-with-falcon is a hieroglyph often used to indicate divine names in writing (glyph 15).

Finally, the Djehutymose coffin uses two kinds of decorative borders to mark scenes and boundaries. By far the most common is the alternating pattern of broad areas of red, blue, green, and white separated by narrow bands of white bounded by black on either side (fig. 124). This pattern is common in Egyptian art in general and in this painted form is a much cheaper substitute for the elaborate inlaid work it represents. Rather less common is the pattern in red at the foot of the coffin base: this geometrical pattern represents woven rushes of a sort used in the earliest Egyptian architecture (fig. 125). Plain colored lines are used to further provide boundaries between scenes, scenes and text, or lines of text: note the use of alternating red and blue lines separating text on the coffin base (as in fig. 123) and interior lid and the use of blue lines only on the lid exterior.

Fig. 122. Nub or gold symbol from coffin lid foot.

Glyph 13

Glyph 14

Glyph 15

Fig. 123. Falcon on standard atop Amentet's head, coffin base interior.

Fig. 125. Patterned border from coffin base exterior.

Fig. 124. Colored border from coffin lid exterior.

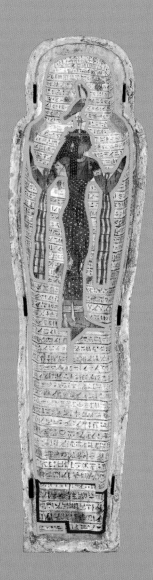

Diagram showing the locations of specific texts on the Djehutymose coffin

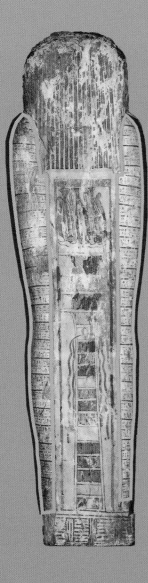

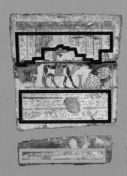

Locations of specific texts on the Djehutymose coffin are outlined in color and identified

1. Nephthys Text

2. Book of the Dead, chapter 9

3. Isis Text

4. Book of the Dead, chapter 9

5. Divine procession texts (derived from Book of the Dead, chapters 151 and 169)

6. "Eye of Horus" Text

7. Book of the Dead, chapter 1

8. Nut Texts

9. Offering Texts

Fig. 126. Fragment from Book of the Dead papyrus showing goddess Ma'at, Ptolemaic Period, 332–30 BC, papyrus, ink, paint (KM 1981.4.22).

Fig. 127. Ma'at amulet, Ptolemaic Period, 332–30 BC, bronze (KM 1971.2.142).

Djehutymose's Afterlife Ambitions

What Djehutymose and his family hoped for after his burial involved different scenarios for the physical and spiritual components of the dead man. Djehutymose's physical remains would ideally stay forever in the tomb where they were put to rest. The presence of a carefully identified and recognizable body was important for Djehutymose's afterlife survival: without it, his spiritual components would have no home base, and he would have no heart to provide memory and testimony in his final judgment. So the preservation of the body and security of its tomb were important, but their roles were relatively passive—they had only to endure.

After death, the active parts of Djehutymose were spiritual: his *ka*, *ba*, shadow, name, and other less well-defined parts were involved in the complex processes of getting Djehutymose from the tomb through the Netherworld, to a final judgment and then beyond that into an afterlife. This was a journey with many pitfalls and dangers: Djehutymose would encounter seemingly endless gates with armed guardians ready to kill him if he missed the answer to a question. Other perils awaited, including the possibility of discouragement, and throughout the way he would be plagued by the uncertainty of his destination, fears that he was entering into a topsy-turvy world where people walked upside down, ate excrement, and drank urine. Assuming that Djehutymose finally made it to his judgment, his ordeal was far from over: he would have to endure a gauntlet of 42 knife-wielding gods, each of whom he would have to address and claim innocence from a particular act—from murder and theft to lying and bad temper. Then he would face a final test: the weighing of his heart, which contained the memory of everything he had ever done, against a feather embodying the Egyptian concept of *ma'at*, which was truth, right, and order, the way things were supposed to be. (Ma'at was often represented as a goddess wearing a feather on her head—figs. 126–127). A hybrid monster, part crocodile, part lion, and part hippopotamus, waited to devour him if he failed. Only if he passed this final test would Djehutymose be declared "true-of-voice" or "justified": he would become an "effective spirit" (Egyptian *akh*) and would be allowed to enter into the afterlife. After the dangers he had just passed, this afterlife might seem tame to us, but it was exactly what Djehutymose and all Egyptians wanted. Set in a place known variously as the "Field of Reeds" or "Field of Offerings" consisting of islands of well-irrigated farmland, this was a paradise for a heavily agricultural society like ancient Egypt, a land of predictable abundance (fig. 128). Djehutymose would pass his time with family, friends, and, most importantly, the gods, in a peaceful, leisured afterlife where all work was carried out by magical servant figures who represented Djehutymose. This afterlife was, to the Egyptians, well worth the expense of preparing for it.

Djehutymose did not go unaided on his journey to the afterlife. The protection for his physical body provided by his coffin and its protective divine images also carried over to his spiritual components. More importantly, the protective texts inscribed on the coffin were intended as a guide, giving him an idea of what to expect and how to deal with the obstacles he encountered. The presence of the texts on the mummy case, separate from Djehutymose's spirit as it made the journey, implies some degree of communication between the tomb and the Netherworld, the ability of the *ba* to return to the tomb to check texts or even the possibility that Djehutymose might have learned or memorized the texts at some point either before or after death. The condition of the texts raises other questions. Some of the texts, especially those relating to the gods on the sides of the coffin, are heavily abridged, other texts are corrupt copies or missing portions, and parts of some texts were hacked away to accommodate Djehutymose's oversized mummy. Did these factors create problems for Djehutymose: are the texts less effective for being incomplete or corrupt? In general it seems not; at least, given the large number of incomplete, imperfect, or damaged copies of the texts in existence, it seems that the intention or the presence of at least part of the text was enough.

But what did these texts say? The majority of texts on the Djehutymose coffin come from the Egyptian Book of the Dead: by Djehutymose's time, this was the standard compilation of funerary texts for private individuals. Not a "book" as a modern reader might understand it, the Book of the Dead (known to the ancient Egyptians as "Coming forth by Day") was a collection of hymns, prayers, texts of mythological exegesis, dialogues, magical spells, and related compositions designed to give the reader a guide to what to expect in the Netherworld and what to do about it. But the Book of the Dead does not present its information in a set narrative sequence: modern readers expecting a consecutive account from burial to judgment to afterlife are invariably disappointed. This is not to say that sequence is unimportant; indeed it was around Djehutymose's lifetime that a major

Fig. 128. Fragment of Book of the Dead papyrus, showing man rowing boat in the Field of Offerings (chapter 110), Ptolemaic Period, 332–30 BC, ink, papyrus (KM 1981.4.24).

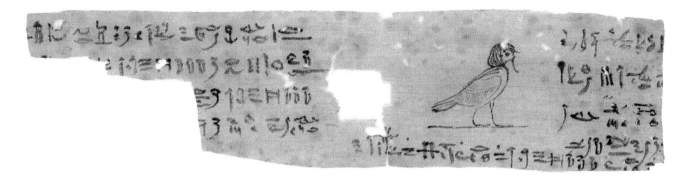

Fig. 129. Mummy bandage inscribed with Book of the Dead texts, Late–Ptolemaic Periods, 525–30 BC, cloth, ink (KM 1971.2.278b).

revision of the text of the Book of the Dead set the order of individual texts to the sequence on which the (modern) chapter numbers are based. Related chapters tend to be grouped together, and one can see a sequential movement between groups of chapters. The Book of the Dead is primarily thought of as a text written at length on a papyrus roll, but the texts were also placed on a wide range of funerary objects as well, and the coffin of Djehutymose includes some of the most important Book of the Dead chapters. The inscription of Book of the Dead chapters on a coffin had the advantage of keeping the text closer to the body—it was harder to lose than a papyrus roll. Indeed, in later periods it became common to inscribe chapters of the Book of the Dead, often with illustrations, onto the bandages wrapping a mummy—providing even more security (although the texts written on linen are often nearly illegible) (fig. 129).

It was impossible to inscribe a complete copy of the Book of the Dead on Djehutymose's coffin, so the selection of texts that would fit onto the coffin was of particular importance. Not only were Book of the Dead texts chosen, but also other texts, some adapted from the Book of the Dead and some from other sources, that were particularly appropriate for a coffin were included as well. Absent a fuller copy of the Book of the Dead on papyrus or mummy bandages, the texts on the coffin gave Djehutymose the essential information he needed after death.[45]

The texts on Djehutymose's coffin are written in a form of the Egyptian language known to scholars as "Middle Egyptian," the "classic" phase of the language but one that was very far removed from the form of Egyptian in use for everyday purposes in Djehutymose's time. Indeed, Middle Egyptian had not been a spoken language for nearly a thousand years by the time it was being written on Djehutymose's coffin. Although the writing system and basic vocabulary survived with relatively little change, the underlying grammar of the language and the "spelling" of many words had changed quite drastically. These texts were in an older form of the language, of course, because the originals themselves were already ancient, hundreds of years old or even older. Even when newly composed, these texts would have contained obscurities, being derived from still earlier texts from sometimes-conflicting traditions. These ancient texts had been copied, over and over, by hand. Over the centuries, errors and misunderstandings crept into the copies, from which further copies would be made, introducing still more errors and changes.

Thus, the scribe copying texts onto Djehutymose's coffin had to face a number of obstacles: texts in an archaic form of the Egyptian language, texts that were probably obscure even in perfect condition, and texts that were by this point mildly to considerably corrupted by copying errors and misunderstandings. So the surprise is not so much that the texts of Djehutymose's coffin contain mistakes and obscurities but that they are comprehensible at all. The modern reader is at an even further remove, reading texts in a dead language that not only suffer from a variety of errors and obscurities but also suffer from damage that has obliterated portions of text. The inscriptions that cover Djehutymose's coffin thus abound in problems, and the translations that follow must be taken as provisional and heavily dependent on earlier scholarship, an initial attempt to make sense of this mass of textual material. (Note that, in the translations that follow, square brackets indicate damaged or illegible passages restored from other sources, parentheses indicate material either restored from other sources or interpolated as explanation, and question marks indicate major uncertainties.)

One can "read" Djehutymose's coffin from top to bottom and, in many ways, this is the most appropriate way to approach the exterior of the coffin lid. The text that accompanies the image of Nephthys on the head of the coffin is heavily damaged, but parallels permit at least the general knowledge that this is a text in which Nephthys promises protection to Djehutymose: "I exist as your protection," the goddess proclaims (fig. 130). Indeed, the utterances of protective goddesses punctuate the lid of the coffin. Farther down, below Djehutymose's head, the goddess Nut spreads her wings and speaks, although the main text accompanying this image is a speech by Djehutymose, derived from Book of the Dead, chapter 9, and

Fig. 130. Portion of damaged Nephthys text, coffin base exterior.

131

132

Fig. 131. Ram god Banebdjedet and associated text.

Fig. 132. Isis text from coffin lid foot.

Fig. 133. Error in Isis text, giving the name of the goddess Nut instead of the similarly spelled name for the "Watery Abyss" Nun.

directed at the ram god Banebdjed represented on either side: "O great ram of dignity: I have come to see, to penetrate into the Netherworld" (fig. 131). Again, the text is damaged and parts are illegible. Over the feet of Djehutymose, the goddess Isis spreads her protective wings and addresses Djehutymose at length (fig. 132):

> I have come and I exist as your protection, Osiris the priest of Horus, priest of the Golden One, Djehutymose, son of the like-titled Nespasefy, justified, born of the mistress of the house Tareru, giving breath to your nose, the North Wind that comes forth from Atum, so that your nose rejoices. [I set] your throat [upright], causing you to exist as a god, your enemies overthrown [beneath] your sandals. May you be justified before Re, may you be strong before the Ennead. I have joined your body, I have secured your ascent (?) so that you will make the journey of Osiris, Foremost of the Westerners. You will be justified in the sky. I will make your protection. I have caused your face to be illuminated in Nut [*sic*], I will open your eyes for you forever. . . .

Note that the scribe has made a number of mistakes in copying this text, not the least of which is the mention of the goddess Nut (glyph 16), which is a mistake for the similarly written Nun (glyph 17), the Watery Abyss out of which the sun-god created himself (fig. 133). The positioning of this text is significant: Egyptologist Maarten Raven has noted that texts relating to journeys often appear on or near the feet of coffins.[46]

In between these protective utterances of goddesses, we find another Book of the Dead text in the lower center of the coffin: the first

133

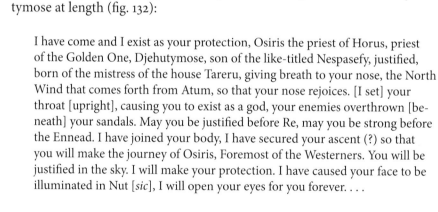

Glyph 16

Glyph 17

134

parts of Book of the Dead, chapter 89, in five columns down the center of the coffin, written in elaborately painted hieroglyphs (fig. 134). This text is usually in this position in later period coffins and is often elaborately colored, sometimes even inlaid in colored glass or stones. This chapter of the Book of the Dead is sometimes given the title "Chapter for causing the *ba* to rejoin its body in the God's Domain" and addresses the fear that a *ba* might abandon or be separated from its body against its will. In papyri, the chapter is often illustrated with an image of the *ba*-bird hovering over a mummy, so the embalming scene above the text does double duty: it shows the embalming of Djehutymose by Anubis but also serves as the illustration for the text below. The text is heavily damaged and incomplete but can be partly reconstructed based on parallels:

> Words spoken by Osiris the priest of Horus, priest of the Golden One, Djehu-tymose, justified, son of the like-titled Nespasefy, born of the mistress of the house Tareru: [O bringer, O runner, who is in] his hall: may you cause my *ba* to come to me from any place where it may be. [If you are slow in bringing my *ba* to me from any place where he might be, you will find the Eye of Horus stand-ing against you like] those Watchers. They will not sleep in Heliopolis, [land of the thousands for the one who is] with him. My *ba* takes for me [the effective spirit that is with] me wherever it may be. Take heed [for yourself: those of the sky belong to] my *ba*. If you are slow in letting me see my *ba* and my corpse, you will find the Eye of Horus standing against you like those. (fig. 135)

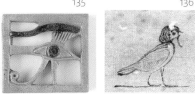
135   136

Note that Djehutymose threatens any being who might keep his *ba* from him (fig. 136); this is a classic Egyptian magical strategy, whereby even gods can be threatened with harm if they are acting contrary to the principles of *ma'at*, the way things are supposed to be.[47]

Flanking this important text, on both sides, are the processions of gods along the sides of the coffin, already described in terms of the gods they represent. Each of the 22 gods shown is accompanied by a short text recording what the gods say, often reflecting what the particular gods will do for Djehutymose to further his afterlife aims. These are set texts typi-cally found in this position on coffins of the Saite Period, and many of the texts are versions of selections from Book of the Dead, chapters 151 and 169. As inscribed on Djehutymose's coffin, these texts are drastically abbrevi-ated, in some cases, to fit the available space. Fuller parallels permit some

Fig. 134. Portion of Book of the Dead, chapter 89, from coffin lid exterior.

Fig. 135. Eye of Horus amulet, Late–Ptolemaic Periods, 525–30 BC, faience (KM 1971.2.29).

Fig. 136. *Ba* bird: detail of mummy bandage in fig. 129.

Fig. 137. Procession of gods from Djehu-tymose's right flank, showing (*left to right*): Atum, Osiris, Imsety, Anubis, Duamutef.

reconstruction of the complete texts and allow restoration of damaged areas, but there are still gaps and the endings of many of the gods' speeches are uncertain.[48]

Procession of gods on Djehutymose's right (fig. 137)

Words spoken by Atum, Lord of the Two Lands of Heliopolis: I ascend from the eternal cavern in the West. I restore the [corpse] of Osiris, the priest of Horus, priest of the Golden One, [Djehutymose] (. . .)

Words spoken by Osiris, Foremost of the W[est]erners: May he give [life to Osiris] the priest of Horus, priest of the Golden One, Djehutymose, born of (the mistress of the house, Tareru). I distinguish him among the gods, I permit him to enter and go forth from the Netherworld like the stars (from the body of Nut).

Words spoken by Imsety: I made healthy [my father] Osiris, the priest of Horus, priest of the Golden One, Djehutymose, born of the mistress of the house Tareru. I pulled together his flesh, I reassembled his limbs (. . .).

Words spoken by Anubis, who-is-in-the-place-of-embalming: I have come near [you, Osiris, the priest of Horus, priest of the Golden One, Djehutymo]se the justified, to fill you with the medjet-oil (which came forth from the Eye of Horus . . .).

Words spoken by Duamutef: I have come near you, Osiris, the priest of Horus, [priest of the Golden One, Djehutymose, the justified.] I have joined (?)my *ba* to Re (and to your corpse. I have protected you from your injury that I may let you stand on your two feet forever).

Words spoken by Geb, hereditary prince of the gods: (I have come in order to see) Osiris the priest of Horus, priest of the Golden One, Djehutymose, justi-fied, [my eldest son and ruler of his fellows . . .].

[Words spoken by Heka]maitef: Osiris, the priest of Horus, priest of the Golden One, Djehutymose, justified: [I am Hekama]itef, I exist as your protec-tion (removing your enemies from you like what I did for Osiris in Webet).

(fig. 138)

[Words spoken by Iryren]efdjesef: Osiris the priest of Horus, priest of the Golden One, Djehutymose, I am [Iryrenefdjesef, I] have come [from the palace carrying a command of Re so that I might protect you].

[Words spoken by] Wepwawet: [I have made right] the road for Osiris [the priest of Horus, priest of the Golden One, Djehutymose,] to any place [he] wants.

Words spoken by Isis, the great, divine mother: I have come before you, Osiris the priest of Horus, priest of the Golden One, [Djehutymose, justified.] (I exist as your protection . . .).

Words spoken by Nephthys [. . . I have come] before you, Osiris, the priest of Horus, priest of the Golden One, [Djehutymose.] (I exist as your protection . . .).

Fig. 138. Procession of gods from Djehutymose's right flank, showing (*left to right*): Iryrenefdjesef, Wepwawet, Isis, Nephthys.

Procession on Djehutymose's left (fig. 139)

Words spoken by Re-Harakhte, the good god, lord of the sky. I have illuminated [the corpse of Osiris like the *ba* of Re in the Netherworld. I put bright]ness in his cavern. He will never perish, Osiris, the priest of Horus, priest of the Golden One, Djehutymose, justified.

Words spoken by Khepri: I cause Osiris, the priest of Horus, priest of the Golden One, Djehutymose, justified, born of Tareru, to come into being with those of later times. I cause him to endure (in the following of Osiris).[49]

Words spoken by Hapi: I have caused Osiris the priest of Horus, priest of the Golden One, Djehutymose, son of the like-titled Nespasefy, born to the mistress of the house Tareru, to be justified in the cemetery like the lords (of the Netherworld, while you are far from the sky like the *ba* of Re among the excellent spirits).

Words spoken by Anubis, Foremost of the Divine Booth: Osiris the priest of Horus, priest of the Golden One, Djehutymose, justified, born of Tareru, I have come before you to heal (your illnesses, to bind your limbs for you and reassemble your bones for you).

Fig. 139. Procession of gods from Djehutymose's left flank, showing (*right to left*): Khepri, Hapy, Anubis, Qebehsenuf, Horus.

Words spoken by Qebehsenuf: I am your son, Osiris, the priest of Horus, priest of the Golden One, Djehutymose, son of the like-titled Nespasefy, justified. I have come so that I might exist as (your protection . . .).

Words spoken by Horus-without-eyes-in-his-forehead: I have come before you, Osiris the priest of Horus, priest of the Golden One, Djehutymose, born of Tareru, justified. I have established (your limbs for you as a god . . .).

(fig. 140)
Words spoken by Kherybaqef: Osiris the priest of Horus, priest of the Golden One, Djehutymose, son of the like-titled Nespasefy, justified, [I have come from the palace carrying a command of the god to protect you . . .]

[Words spoken by Shu]: I attend to you, Osiris, the priest of Horus, priest of the Golden One, Djehutymose [. . . in front of the one who concealed the plan. I gave breath to your nostrils . . .]

[Words spoken by Tefnut]: [. . .] Osiris the priest of Horus, priest of the Golden One, Djehutymose [. . .]

[Words spoken by Neith:] Come, my son. I smooth over the beauty of [Osiris the priest of Horus, priest of the Golden One, Djehutymose . . .].[50]

[Words spoken by Serqet]: I have given good [offerings] to Osiris, the priest of Horus, priest of the Golden One, [Djehutymose . . .].

Finally, the foot of the coffin, with its representation of the Apis bull and the *ba* bird, is accompanied by a text that does not explicitly refer to either but which relates to the image and the general idea these figures raise (fig. 141).[51] The text concerns the dead person's desire for mobility and access:

Words spoken by Osiris, the priest of Horus, priest of the Golden One, Djehutymose, justified, son of the like-titled Nespasefy, who was made by the mistress of the house Tareru, justified: Open! One opened and one sealed what was sealed and opened to enter and come forth through it. May one open for me the gates in [. . .] O guardian . . . [I am] one who is with you. May you make for me a way so that I might enter . . . .

Fig. 140. Procession of gods from Djehutymose's left flank, showing (*right to left*): Kherybaqef, Shu, Tefnut.

Fig. 141. Scene from foot of coffin lid, showing the Apis bull approaching an offering stand before a tomb, with a *ba* bird hovering above.

Throughout his journey to his final judgment, Djehutymose would encounter gates with guardians and sealed doors. This text helps guarantee his access and his ability to move freely. Thus the text obliquely relates to the illustration: the Apis bull, striding toward a tomb in this case and often shown on later coffins carrying the mummy of the deceased on his back, is a sign of mobility and a need for the ability to enter and go forth from the tomb. The *ba*, as the most mobile part of Djehutymose after death, is also vitally concerned with access and the ability to enter and leave the tomb at will. In illustrated copies of the Book of the Dead on papyrus, the *ba* is often represented near or going through doors, and these images reflect the overall concerns of the Egyptians with the *ba*'s mobility after death. Thus, between this text and the one above, Djehutymose both ensures that he will not be separated from his *ba* and also guarantees the *ba*'s ability to move freely.

These texts on the exterior of the coffin lid all promise protection to Djehutymose and address some of his potential concerns about the afterlife (such as being separated from his *ba* and the *ba*'s mobility). But these exterior inscriptions do not really get at the heart of what Djehutymose was facing: his examination and judgment resulting in his being declared "justified" or "true of voice," his transformation into an effective spirit, and his admission into the afterlife. At least some of the specifics of what Djehutymose would encounter and need are dealt with by the texts on the interior and base of the coffin.

By far the most important text for Djehutymose was Book of the Dead, chapter 1. It is repeated, almost in its entirety, twice on the base of the coffin: once on the interior around the image of Amentet and once on the exterior in the horizontal bands of inscription flanking the image of the Djed pillar. Further, the opening words of the text appear a third time on the coffin base at the foot; when the coffin was closed, the opening of Book of the Dead, chapter 1, "Hail to you, Bull of the West, so says Thoth, king of Eternity . . ." would have appeared below the Apis bull image on the foot and its text, with its references to sealing and opening. Thus, Book of the Dead, chapter 1, encloses Djehutymose on all sides.

Although the chapter numbers in the Book of the Dead are modern designations based on the set order of texts developed in the Saite Period, chapter 1 was important enough to be at, or near, the beginning of many copies of the Book of the Dead from its earliest manifestations. In

142

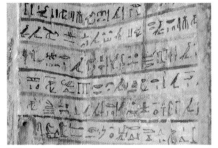

143

144

Fig. 142. Thoth amulet, Ptolemaic Period, 332–30 BC, faience (KM 1971.2.83)

Fig. 143. Detail of text of Book of the Dead, chapter 1, from coffin base interior.

Fig. 144. Detail of text of Book of the Dead, chapter 1, from coffin base exterior, with portions of an offering text on edge of coffin.

papyrus copies, chapter 1 is often accompanied by an illustration showing an elite funerary procession, underlining its primary significance for the most immediate concerns of the recently dead and buried Djehutymose. But its prominence should not lead modern readers to expect a clear-cut narrative progression from this text: this was not the Egyptian way, and very specifically not the way of the texts of the Book of the Dead, which are oblique, elliptical, and filled with obscure allusions through which they convey information needed by the dead person. Instead of the straightforward narrative that a modern reader might want, describing what Djehutymose will encounter after death, the text is a long address to the god Osiris, in which the god Thoth frequently interjects (fig. 142). Djehutymose repeatedly identifies himself with Osiris and Horus, supported by Thoth, and alludes to mythological events involving the gods. Beyond this, Djehutymose repeatedly asks the gods to help him join Osiris, to become part of his domain in the land of the dead.

What follows is a translation of the text of the parts of Book of the Dead, chapter 1, that appear on Djehutymose's coffin, combining the text from the coffin base exterior with that of the base interior (which is better for the later parts of the text). The translation is the text as it appears on the coffin, although some interpolations and corrections have been made from older and better copies of this text. The intention, however, is to give the text as Djehutymose might have read it on his coffin. For ease of reading, the text has been divided into paragraphs along the division suggested for the Saite recension of this chapter by T. G. Allen (figs. 143–144).[52]

[Words spoken by Osiris, the Priest of Horus and Priest of the Golden One, Djehutymose,] justified, son of [the like-titled Nespasefy, justified, born of the] mistress of the house Tareru, [justified]:

Hail to you, Osiris, Bull of the West, so says Thoth, king of Eternity, I am the great God beside the god (in the boat) (fig. 145). I have fought for you (for) I am one of these gods of the magistrates who vindicated Osiris against his enemies on this day of judgment. I belong to your associates, Osiris: I am one of these gods, born of Nut, who slaughters the enemies of Re, who imprisoned those who rebelled against him. I belong to your associates, Horus, I fought for you and I watched over your name.

Fig. 145. Gods riding in a divine boat from a coffin panel, 21st–22nd Dynasty, c. 1000–800 BC, wood, paint, varnish (KM 1981.4.5).

Fig. 146. Text of Book of the Dead, chapter 1, from coffin base exterior, surrounding the Djed pillar.

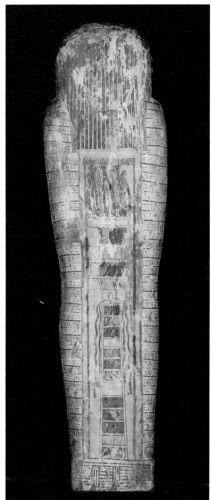

I am Thoth who vindicates Horus against his enemies on this day of judgment in the great palace of the great one in Heliopolis. I am one from Busiris, son of one from Busiris, I being conceived in Pe, I being born in Busiris, otherwise said, Dep. I am with the mourning women who buried Osiris, who lament Osiris on the shores of the washermen. Justify Osiris against his enemies, so says he. Re has protected him, so says Thoth.

I am with the Child (Horus) on this day of clothing the Crushed One, of the opening of the caverns, of the washing of the weary-hearted one, who makes secret the secret things of Rosetjau, so that I might be with Horus as the protector of this left arm of Osiris, who is in Letopolis. I will go forth and I will enter with the Devouring Flame on the day of subduing the rebels in Letopolis, (so that I might be with Horus) on the day of Osiris Wennefer, in order to make offerings to Re on the day of the Sixth-Day Festival and the [Denit Festival] in Heliopolis.

(fig. 146)
I am the *wab*-priest in Busiris, a wise one in Abydos, one who raises the land. I am (one who sees) the secret things in Rosetjau. I am the one who reads the ritual book for the *ba* of Busiris. I am the *setem*-priest in what pertains to him. I am the craftsman on the day of putting the boat of Sokar onto its sledge. I am the one who receives the hoe on the day of hacking up the earth at Herakleopolis.

Fig. 147. Text of Book of the Dead, chapter 1, from coffin base interior, surrounding the goddess Amentet.

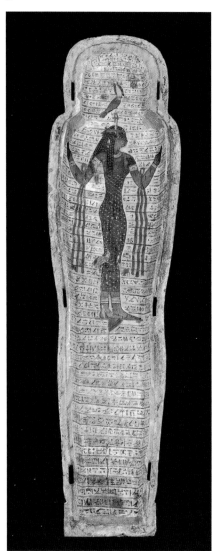

O you who cause the excellent *ba*s to approach the house of Osiris, may you cause the *ba* of Osiris, the Priest of Horus and Priest of the Golden One, Djehutymose, justified, son of the like-titled Nespasefy, justified, born of the mistress of the house Tareru, justified, to approach with you to the house of Osiris. (May he see) as you see, may he hear as you hear, may he stand as you stand, may he sit as you sit. O you who give bread and beer to the excellent *ba*s in the house of Osiris, may you give bread and beer to the *ba* of Osiris, the Priest of Horus and Priest of the Golden One, Djehutymose, justified, son of the priest of Horus of Edfu, [priest of the golden one, priest of] Heliopolis Nespasefy, justified, born of the mistress of the house Tareru, justified, together with you. O you who open the ways and who open up the roads for the excellent *ba*s of the House of Osiris Wennefer, (may you open the ways and open up the roads for Osiris), the Priest of Horus and Priest of the Golden One, Djehutymose, justified, son of the like-titled Nespasefy, justified, born of the mistress of the house Tareru, justified, together with you. May he enter by traversing, may he come forth in peace, may Osiris come forth without him being opposed and without being turned back (from) the house of Osiris. May he come forth and may he enter being praised, may he come forth as his heart desires for him. May one do for him his commands in the House of Osiris. May he go and may he speak with you, Osiris, the priest of Horus and priest of the Golden One, Djehutymose, justified, son of the Priest of Horus of Edfu, Priest of Heliopolis, Nespasefy, justified and born of the mistress of the house, Tareru, justified, goes to the west in peace, without his fault being found in the balance, without one knowing it.

(fig. 147)
I am examined by many mouths. His *ba* is set up before his heart (?), which has found that (my?) speech is sound. See me before you, Lord of the gods, after I have reached the pool of the two truths. I have appeared as a living god and I am shining like the Ennead that is in the sky. I exist like one who is with you. My strides are exalted in Kher-aha, as I see the noble Orion and make whole the Watery Abyss. I am not turned back, I see the Netherworld and smell the provisions of the Ennead, as I sit with them. The lector-priest summons a box for me, I hear the offering list (being read). I walk with the Neshmet-boat, without me being turned back, (my *ba* being with its lord).

Hail to you, Foremost of the Westerners, Osiris, in the Abydos nome, may you cause that I proceed to the West in peace. May the lords of the sacred land receive me, may they speak very highly of me, in peace. May they make a place for me at the side of the elders of the king's council. May the Nurse receive me at all times. I will come forth in the presence of Wennefer, I will follow Horus in Rosetjau, Osiris in Busiris. I will take on any form that my heart desires for Osiris, the priest of Horus and priest of the Golden One, Djehutymose, justified, son of the like-titled Nespasefy, justified and born of the mistress of the house, Tareru.

So the text begins by hailing Osiris as the Bull of the West, an allusion to his potency as well as his position in the funerary direction. Djehutymose, backed up by interjections from Thoth, attests to his own fighting on behalf of Osiris and his son Horus, and claims a place among the gods' associates, in parallel passages. Djehutymose claims Busiris, the town of Osiris, as his birthplace and his father's birthplace, thus claiming further ties to the god and his family. Djehutymose places himself into mythological time, claiming to be present with the mourners for the dead Osiris, and the embalming and burial of Osiris. These events are alluded to only very obliquely—"washing the weary-hearted one" and "clothing the Crushed one" refer to the embalming of Osiris, while "opening the caverns" may be an allusion to his burial. The Egyptians were extremely reluctant to describe or even mention the events surrounding the death of Osiris, so these roundabout allusions are typical. Indeed, the chapter is full of sometimes cryptic allusions to mythic events and persons that serve as reminders to Djehutymose: he will have to face many beings who will quiz him on obscure mythological facts, and the Book of the Dead abounds in references to such information to help the dead person pass such interrogations. But the chapter is not just a crib-sheet for Djehutymose. Djehutymose takes on many identities in these passages: he acts as many different kinds of priests in different rituals (although none of these roles relates to his lifetime duties as priest of Horus of Edfu). His goal is to approach the house of Osiris, the domain of the dead, and he asks the gods to allow this and to let him see, hear, stand, and sit like Osiris. Djehutymose also asks for offerings (which will be promised to him in other texts elsewhere on the coffin) and asks that his paths to the afterlife be clear and unobstructed. He wants to be accepted by the gods and to have freedom of movement and access. But before these things can be done, Djehutymose must pass the final judgment in which he is cross-examined by the gods and his heart weighed. This judgment is alluded

Map showing sacred places mentioned in Book of the Dead, chapter 1

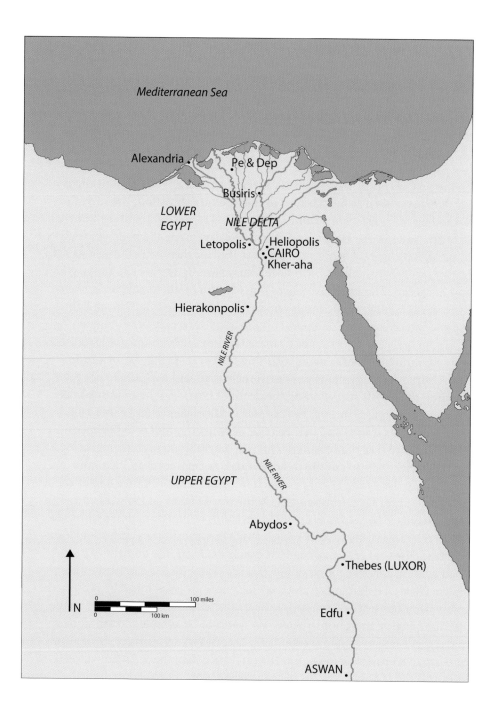

Mediterranean Sea

Alexandria •

Pe & Dep

Busiris •

LOWER
EGYPT

NILE DELTA

Letopolis •

Heliopolis
• •CAIRO
Kher-aha

Hierakonpolis •

NILE RIVER

UPPER EGYPT

NILE RIVER

Abydos •

• Thebes (LUXOR)

N

0   100 miles
0   100 km

Edfu •

ASWAN •

to rather obliquely: "I am examined by many mouths," all of which will ultimately find that "my speech is sound." The result is that Djehutymose appears like a living god, shining like the Ennead (headed, after all, by a sun-god). Djehutymose passes his judgment and is allowed into the afterlife, but the descriptions are allusive and nonsequential, as is customary in the Book of the Dead, indeed in all Egyptian funerary literature.

Book of the Dead, chapter 1, as represented on the Djehutymose coffin is striking in part because of the number of references to places—in his speeches, Djehutymose again and again mentions place names, often situating himself in the place or otherwise connecting himself with it.[53] One might expect references to places in and near Edfu in the south of Egypt, but in fact the places cited are nearly all in the north. Ancient Egypt was divided along north-south lines into **Lower Egypt** (north) and **Upper Egypt** (south), running perpendicular to the axis of the **Nile River**, the central "highway" of transportation in Egypt as well as the literal and conceptual center of Egypt. Somewhat confusingly for those of us used to maps that show north at the top, these modern designations relate to the flow of the Nile River from south to north. So Upper Egypt is in the south, where Edfu and Thebes are located, while Lower Egypt is in the north, the direction toward which the Nile flows, terminating in a number of branches in a marshy area known as the **Delta**, beyond which the river ultimately empties into the Mediterranean Sea. The places in Lower Egypt that Book of the Dead, chapter 1, references are extremely ancient towns and cities with histories that reach back into Egypt's Predynastic Period of political unification and consolidation, and also places of deep mythological significance. Most often mentioned is **Busiris,** located in the central Nile Delta. Busiris was a major cult center for the god Osiris, particularly associated with the Djed pillar as the backbone of Osiris, and Djehutymose identifies himself as having been born in Busiris as the son of a Busirite, underlining his identification with Osiris (fig. 148). Djehutymose's connections to Busiris are intertwined with his relationships to the twin towns of **Pe** and **Dep**. Indeed we get alternate readings in the two copies of Book of the Dead, chapter 1. Both versions describe Djehutymose as being conceived in Pe; the coffin interior version describes him as being born in Dep, while the exterior version tempers this, describing his being born "in Busiris, otherwise said, Dep," the classic way in which Egyptian texts account for the multiple realities caused by variant local traditions. Pe and Dep were celebrated as the twin capitals

Fig. 148. Djed pillar amulet, Ptolemaic Period, 332–30 BC, Terenouthis, Egypt, carnelian (KM 24202).

Fig. 149. Snake coffin, Late–Ptolemaic Periods, 525–30 BC, bronze (KM 4673).

of Predynastic Lower Egypt, eventually consolidating as the town of Buto, major cult center for the snake goddess Wadjyt, one of the two goddesses of kingship over the two parts of Egypt (fig. 149). With both Osiris and his son Horus as legendary kings of Egypt, the reference makes sense in the context of Djehutymose's identification with Osiris. Djehutymose also identifies himself with Horus, and does so with reference to the town of **Letopolis**, a major Delta cult center of Horus. Further associations with Horus can be seen in the reference to Djehutymose's strides being exalted in **Kher-aha**, the site of a major mythological battle between Horus and Seth; Kher-aha ultimately became a place of great significance in Egyptian history—a major fortification in the Roman Period known as "Babylon" that eventually became the old part of the city that would be known as Cairo, the medieval and modern capital of Egypt. To the north of Kher-aha lay **Heliopolis**, the ancient center of solar worship, where Djehutymose's father had a priestly office: in the context of Book of the Dead, chapter 1, Djehutymose promises to make offering at specific named festivals in Heliopolis.

Book of the Dead, chapter 1, does reference a few places farther south in Upper Egypt. Most important, certainly, is the mention of **Abydos**: with Busiris, Abydos was one of the two major cult centers for Osiris. Indeed, by Djehutymose's time, Abydos had come to be central to Egyptian understandings of the afterlife and was a major mortuary landscape of great complexity and antiquity. (The University of Michigan's field project at Abydos, headed by Janet Richards, has done much to explicate the subtleties of this mortuary landscape, fig. 150) The pairing of Busiris (in Lower Egypt) and Abydos (in Upper Egypt) in this text allows Djehutymose to place himself in the two major cult centers of Osiris; Busiris dominates the text, but Abydos was much closer to Djehutymose in Edfu (in life) and Nag el-Hassiya (in burial). Of the two, Djehutymose is most likely to have visited Abydos in his lifetime, as it was not far from Dendera, which Djehutymose almost certainly would have visited in his professional capacity. Farther north from Abydos, the town of **Herakleopolis** is mentioned in the text in a mythological allusion: Djehutymose is given the hoe on the day of hacking up the earth at Herakleopolis—an ancient ritual mentioned in a number of other sources. Herakleopolis is known in Egyptian history primarily for being the capital of the Dynasty 9–10 kings in the First Intermediate Period but was also very active in Djehutymose's time. Thebes, the important political and religious center, is not mentioned at all. Djehutymose's town,

Edfu, of course, is frequently mentioned in the text with each repetition of Djehutymose's fuller titles but does not feature in the complex mythological and historical landscape of the text.

Beyond these earthly places, Book of the Dead, chapter 1, and the other texts on Djehutymose's coffin reference a number of other places not likely to be found on any map of Egypt. The frequently mentioned **Rosetjau** did, at one point in Egyptian history, refer to an actual location, the cemeteries at Giza. But, by the time of the composition of Book of the Dead, chapter 1, Rosetjau had become, instead, a general term for "cemetery" or "necropolis," or even a kind of idealized concept of *the cemetery*. Thus when Djehutymose speaks of being one who sees "the secret things in Rosetjau," he could be referring specifically to his own cemetery at Nag el-Hassiya, or to cemeteries in general, or both—such references are often multivalent. The cemetery, as mentioned before, is in the **West**, whether literally (and this is ideal) or metaphorically, the West being the funerary direction par excellence. From the West, one goes to the **Netherworld** (Egyptian: *Duat*). The Netherworld is the mysterious region where the sun goes at night; stars can pass through it, but it is not directly visible from the earth. The Egyptians were fascinated by the topography of this region, and many images of the

Fig. 151. Papyrus showing part of Egyptian vision of the Netherworld: Book of Amduat, 12th Hour; 21st–22nd Dynasty, c. 1000–800 BC, papyrus, ink (KM 1974.1.1).

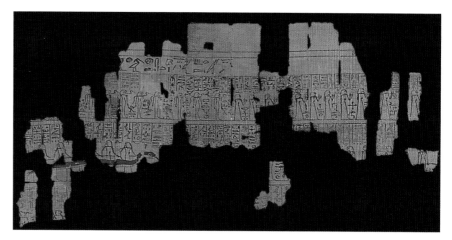

Netherworld and its inhabitants appear in a number of religious compositions (fig. 151). The Netherworld arose from **Nun**, the Watery Abyss below the earth, the nothingness from which creation arose (and, thanks to Egyptian notions of cyclical time, from which creation was constantly re-arising). The Netherworld is the kingdom of Osiris and the domain through which the dead must pass, populated by gods but also hostile beings that pose dangers to the dead. The Netherworld is filled with paths and roads, blocked by doors and gates, often guarded by fierce beings wielding weapons: the dead must correctly answer any questions posed to them for access or be stopped forever in their progress. In contrast to the murky uncertainties of the Netherworld is the **sky**; the Egyptian word (*pet*) is often translated "heaven," but this is, in some ways, a theologically loaded term in English and may best be avoided in talking of the ancient Egyptians. The sky is the domain of the sun-god, who daily takes his boat across it in an arc above the surface of the earth, the place through which stars and other celestial beings travel as well. The sky, in some distant region, is also where the afterlife destinations of the dead lay: the **Field of Reeds** and **Field of Offerings** are located in the sky and were the goal accessible only to those dead who have passed their final judgment, been declared "justified" or "true of voice," and have become "effective spirits." So, although the Netherworld is Djehutymose's immediate destination after death, his ultimate goal involved reaching loftier realms.

The sky, of course, can also be seen in its personification by the sky-goddess Nut in the coffin interior, and this representation is surrounded by texts that are speeches by Nut or texts otherwise relating to her in some way. These texts are a mixture of Book of the Dead, chapter 169, and a set of texts specific to coffins of this period, given with some repetition and variation.[54] These texts emphasize Nut's role as divine mother and, by extension, protector of Djehutymose (fig. 152).

> Words spoken by Nut, the great one, mother of the gods: Hail Osiris, the priest of Horus and priest of the Golden One, Djehutymose, justified, son of the like-titled Nespasefy, justified and born of the mistress of the house, Tareru, justified. Your *ba* is in the sky, your corpse is in the Netherworld. Bread is in your belly, water is in your throat, and the breath of life in your nose, Osiris, the priest of Horus and priest of the Golden One, Djehutymose, justified, son of the like-titled Nespasefy, justified and born of the mistress of the house, Tareru, justified, forever. May you rest with those who are in their shrines, forever, Osiris, the priest of Horus and priest of the Golden One, Djehutymose, justified, son of the like-titled Nespasefy, justified and born of the mistress of the house, Tareru, justified, [forever. Words spoken by Nut: Hail, Osiris, the priest of Horus and priest of the Golden One, Djehutymose, justified, son of the priest of Horus and priest of] the Golden One Nes[pasefy, justified and born of the mistress of the house], Tareru, justified. I conceived [you in] Lower Egypt (and I bore you in Upper Egypt.) I am your mother Nut. I am your protection. I hid your place in the mound of judgment beside the great god who gives you (?) to the West. You rest in the shadow of the noble Ished tree on this day when Re made them content. I have caused that you ascend to the sky so that you may join the horizon. When you travel, Re rejoices every day. Osiris, the priest of Horus and priest of the Golden One, Djehutymose, justified, son of the like-titled Nespasefy, justified and born of the mistress of the house, Tareru, justified: Geb inherits (his) desire, as your protection on your day (?) in order to overthrow his enemies. May you attain your respect like what he does for his father. Osiris, the priest of Horus and priest of the Golden One, Djehutymose, justified, son of the like-titled Nespasefy, justified and born of the mistress of the house, Tareru, justified. . . .

The text shifts to a speech of Geb, Nut's husband, but quickly reverts back to Nut as speaker and includes some repetition of text presented earlier:

> Words spoken by Geb, divine hereditary prince: Hail Osiris, the priest of Horus and priest of the Golden One, Djehutymose, justified, son of the

Fig. 152. Nut texts from coffin lid interior, surrounding the goddess Nut.

like-titled Nespasefy, justified and born of the mistress of the house, Tareru, justified. (I) open for you your blind eyes, I stretch out for you (your) contracted (feet). You are given your heart of your mother, your breast of your body. Your soul is (to) the sky, your corpse (to) the Netherworld. Words spoken by Nut, the Great One, who bore the gods: this son, Osiris, the priest of Horus and priest of the Golden One, Djehutymose, justified, I conceived you in Lower Egypt and I gave birth to you in Upper Egypt. I am your mother Nut. I am your protection. I hid your place in the mound of judgment, beside the great god who gives you (?) to the West. You rest in the shadow of the noble Ished tree on this day when Re made them content (?). I have caused that you ascend to the sky so that you may join the horizon. When you travel, Re rejoices [every day . . . Osiris, the priest of Horus and priest of the Golden One, Djehutymose, justified,] son of the like-titled Nespasefy, justified and born of the mistress of the house, Tareru, justified: Geb inherits what (he) desires (?) forever.

Up front, we get a basic statement about Djehutymose's ambitions: "Your *ba* is in the sky, your corpse is in the Netherworld. Bread is in your belly, water is in your throat, and the breath of life in your nose." This is where and how Djehutymose wants to be: his physical body under the protection of Osiris, while his spirit is free to travel and go to the afterlife places in the sky, being sated and satisfied, and breathing—which is to say, living—after death. Nut identifies herself explicitly as Djehutymose's mother and protector, giving him shade in the shadow of the Ished tree (a sacred tree at Heliopolis) and causing him to go up the sky and travel around. Note that the goddess describes Djehutymose as being conceived in Lower Egypt and born in Upper Egypt—in doing so she connects the dead man with both parts of Egypt and, by implication, each part's sacred places and gods. The statements of Nut are important enough that they are repeated twice—at the head and foot of the lid interior, with the final speeches trailing onto the side of the coffin. In between them are interjected a few other texts, most notably a speech of the god Geb, Nut's husband, adapted from Book of the Dead, chapter 169. Geb, as the god of the earth, addresses Djehutymose's earthly form, concerning himself with the state of Djehutymose's dead body. Thus he says that he will open Djehutymose's blind eyes, straighten out his contracted feet, and take care of both his heart, containing his intelligence and memory, and the bodily chest that contains it. He concludes with the same promise as Nut about the disposition of Djehutymose's *ba* to the sky and his corpse to the Netherworld. Between them, Nut and Geb care for Djehutymose's physical and spiritual components, but Nut's concerns predominate in this text around her image.

The Nut texts on the coffin lid interior lead directly into another important group of texts: offering texts, intended to guarantee offerings for the dead person in the afterlife. These texts are highly formulaic and, as such, often treated in a cursory way. But the formula used is both important and extremely common—the majority of Egyptian objects in museums are inscribed with some variation on this formula—and the details can be revealing. The formula is instantly recognizable by its beginning (glyphs 18), usually rendered "hetep-di-nesu," "An offering that the king gives" or "A royal offering."[55] By far the most common version of this formula adds the god Osiris as agent, the god through whom the royal offering is made, so "A royal offering of Osiris," often followed by the god's titles. The offerings can be, and often are, enumerated, but even if not, this formula is followed by the name of the beneficiary, plus titles and parentage if space permitted. This very basic formula we have seen already on the Ptah-Sokar-Osiris statues from the Djehutymose family.

Glyphs 18. The beginning of the standard offering formula.

More elaborate examples of the offering formula appear on the coffin of Djehutymose. Although damaged, one such inscription (from the right side of the exterior of the base of the coffin) sums up Djehutymose's desires very nicely:

> [A royal offering of Osiris,] Foremost of the westerners, Lord of Abydos: may he give invocation offerings consisting of cattle and fowl and every good and pure thing and every pleasant thing. May he give a thousand of bread, may he give a thousand of beer, may he give a thousand of wine, may he give a thousand of milk, may he give a thousand of incense, may he give a beautiful burial in the beautiful West for the *ka* of Osiris, the priest of Horus and priest of the Golden One, Djehutymose, son of the like-titled Nespasefy, son of Nakhthor, justified and born of the mistress of the house, Tareru, justified.

The facing side of the coffin invokes royal offerings from a wider variety of gods, going down the hierarchy from sun-gods to the four sons of Horus:

> A royal offering of [. . .], Atum . . . [. . . Imsety, Hapy, Duamu]tef, Qebehsenuf, Isis and Nephthys: may they give offerings and provisions (consisting of) every

good and pure thing and every pleasant thing. May he give a thousand of bread, may he give a thousand of beer, may he give a thousand of linen (to the *ka* of) Osiris, the priest of Horus and priest of the Golden One, Djehutymose, born of the mistress of the house Tareru.

A third offering text appears on the interior of the coffin base, beneath the feet of the goddess Amentet just after the text of Book of the Dead, chapter 1, likewise invoking offerings of Re-Harakhte (fig. 153):

Fig. 153. Offering text from coffin base interior.

> A royal offering of Re-Harakhte, Great God, Lord of the Sky, who illuminates the Two Lands, may he give invocation offerings of cattle, fowl and every good and pure thing, everything; may he give offerings and provisions, may he give a thousand loaves of bread and (jugs of) beer, may he give a thousand (jars) of wine, may he give a thousand (jars) of milk, may he give a thousand (pieces of) linen, may he give a beautiful burial in the midst of the West at Edfu for the priest of Horus and priest of the Golden One, Djehutymose, justified, son of the like-titled Nespasefy, justified and born of the mistress of the house, Tareru, justified.

On the interior of the coffin lid, two offering texts flank the goddess Nut on either side. One is for a royal offering specifically attributed to the sun-god Re-Harakhte, while the other involves a range of gods as on the exterior:

> A royal offering of Re-Harakhte, great god, lord of the sky, who illuminates the two lands: what one makes for you (?), Osiris, the priest of Horus and priest of the Golden One, Djehutymose, justified, son of the like-titled Nespasefy, justified and born of the mistress of the house, Ta(reru, justified.)
> (fig. 154)
> A royal offering of Osiris, Foremost of the Westerners, the Great God, Lord of Abydos, [. . .] Khepri, who created (himself), Geb, hereditary prince of

Fig. 154. Offering text from coffin lid interior.

the gods, Imsety, Hapi, Duamutef, Qebehsenuf, Isis, Nephthys: may they give invocation-offerings consisting of bread, beer, cattle, fowl, and every good and pure thing, everything that is given for a good burial to Osiris, the priest of Horus and priest of the Golden One, Djehutymose, justified, son of the like-titled Nespasefy, justified.

The specifics of the offerings are important in what they tell us about the ancient Egyptians and their needs and expectations. Bread and beer were the staples of life in ancient Egypt: made from emmer and barley, the growing of which dictated the entire agricultural economy of Egypt, these two items were at the heart of the Egyptian diet across the economic scale. The beef and poultry were the most desirable of meats in a land where meat was a relative luxury and where most people would have gotten such animal proteins as they would get from the much cheaper and more plentiful fish. Together, the bread, beer, and flesh made up the basics of the Egyptian diet, heavy in starches, carbohydrates, somewhat less so in proteins. Some of the texts also call for wine and milk, further luxuries for most Egyptians but something more a matter of course to someone of Djehutymose's class. The Egyptian diet did include vegetables and fruits, nuts and seeds, oils and fats, but these were not specifically listed in these offering formulas, although they were sometimes represented in scenes of offerings. These unspecified foods could be covered by the generic phrase "offerings and provisions" found in some of the offering texts. Note that some of the texts specify quantities: "a thousand of . . ." This amount is not necessarily to be taken literally but simply implies an abundance beyond what anyone could consume at any one time. This abundance is an important part of the Egyptians' understanding of the afterlife as the complete fulfillment of earthly needs in an agricultural paradise.

One of Djehutymose's offering texts also promises "a thousand (pieces of) linen" (fig. 155). This abundance of cloth may be to fill an earthly need: the Egyptians certainly prized fine linen for clothing, the quality and amount of which could be a status marker for Djehutymose. But linen cloth

Fig. 155. Detail of offering text: portion referring to the offering of cloth.

Fig. 156. Mummy bandages from child mummy in fig. 159.

was also needed for another purpose that was, at the time of Djehutymose's death, much more urgent: cloth for the bandaging of Djehutymose's mummy (fig. 156). Large amounts of linen would be used for bandaging, the finer and newer the better, although household linens could also be repurposed (and often were, as indicated by laundry marks on mummy bandages made from bedsheets).[56] So the needs for cloth would have been twofold: clothing for the afterlife but also bandages for the more immediate needs of mummification. This is in line with another item in the lists of offerings: incense, which would have been useful in the context of a funeral ceremony. And three of Djehutymose's offering texts ask for some variation on a "beautiful burial," "in the midst of the West of Edfu," "in the beautiful West" and "everything that is given" for such a burial.[57] "The West of Edfu" is a specific reference to the cemetery of Nag el-Hassiya; again, "the West" is the funerary direction, not necessarily literal, where burials take place.

Djehutymose's offering texts illustrate one of the Egyptians' favorite literary forms: the list. From the highest of literature and the most reverent of religious texts to the most humble memorandum, Egyptian texts of all levels are full of lists. To the Egyptians, listing things helped control and order them, important in a culture where the maintenance of order was a primary goal. But compiling a list left the danger of leaving something out, and in the world of afterlife wishes and offering texts the possibility of accidental omission was a particular concern. The Egyptians were a practical people, however, and offering formula lists usually included some phrase designed to cover all possibilities and to take care of inadvertent omissions. Thus the lists of offerings conclude with phrases like "and every good and pure thing," "and every pleasant thing," even simply "everything" or "everything that is usually done for" someone or something. These simple phrases reflect aspects of Egyptian thinking, in their emphasis on "good" and "pleasant" things, and, more particularly, in their emphasis on things that are usually done—the Egyptian respect for social norms and conventions being especially strong in a funerary context. The repeated emphasis on things being "pure" may reflect Egyptian concerns for ritual purity (important for a priest like Djehutymose) but more basically represent realities of Egyptian life, where purity of food and drink would be a special concern, given the general levels of hygiene available to the Egyptians. The great fear of an upside-down world in the afterlife in which the dead might have to eat feces or drink urine surely underlies at least some of the offering texts' concerns for purity as well.

These offering texts function as magical providers of offerings for the dead: the mere fact of their being initially written, and any subsequent reading of the texts, magically brings the offerings into being. Thus the repetition of these texts on Djehutymose's coffin and Ptah-Sokar-Osiris figure provides multiple opportunities for the generation of offerings and backups in case an offering text is damaged or lost. Note the references to "invocation offerings," literally "voice-offerings": these refer to offerings whose existence is brought into being by being spoken aloud. So the bread, beer, cattle, fowl, etc. listed afterward are magically brought into being by the mere act of speaking their names as well. All over the coffin, Djehutymose is being provided with offerings and provisions for both his burial and his afterlife.

Another very important feature of the textual program of the coffin is the extensive repetition of Djehutymose's name and titles and his parents' names and titles throughout (glyphs 19). These appear in every individual inscription, and in some cases appear many times over. In fact, this repeated information makes up roughly a sixth of the total inscription of the coffin: Djehutymose's own names and titles appear some 58 times on the coffin, while those of his father and mother appear more than 30 times (and his grandfather is named once). As mentioned above, the identification of the coffin with Djehuytmose's name was important to ensure that his *ba* and *ka* could identify his body. But the name was important in an even more basic way as an integral part of Djehutymose's personal identity: it was an essential part of who Djehutymose was. Indeed, the name functions almost as another spiritual component of the dead man: its written repetition on the coffin and in other inscriptions mirrors the oral repetition of the name in funeral rituals and the spoken offering prayers that were an important part of the acts performed by the survivors on behalf of the dead person.

Thus the repetition of the name Djehutymose all over the coffin is understandable: part identifier, part identity, and part commemoration of the deceased. The repetition of Djehutymose's titles is also understandable: since he was a member of the priestly elite, his life and identity were bound up in his official positions—these further served to identify and honor the dead man. The frequent repetition of Djehutymose's parents' names and titles is a part of his overall identification with his family and class but also served an immediately practical function: the name Djehutymose had been

Glyphs 19. Djehutymose's name and titles.

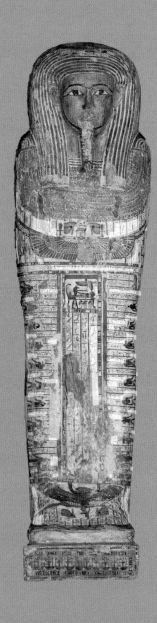

Diagram locating all occurrences of Djehutymose's name and titles on his coffin

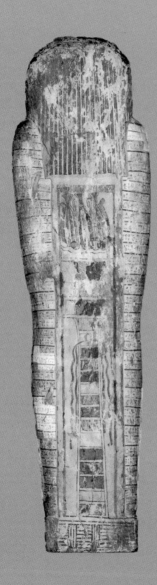

DJEHUTYMOSE'S NAME

Occurrences of the name and titles of Djehutymose and his family on the coffin are highlighted in yellow

Fig. 157. Djehutymose identified by his mother's name (and note correction in text): Djehutymose coffin.

relatively common in Egypt since the New Kingdom, so these added identifiers specify *which* Djehutymose is meant out of the thousands of Egyptians who would have borne that name. The use of both father and mother in these identifiers shows the Egyptians' understandings of the roles of both parents in the identities of their children and something of the relative status of men and women in Egyptian society. Indeed, in the few cases where Djehutymose is identified by the name of only one parent, it is more often that of his mother Tareru alone than his father. Identification by mother's name is a fairly common practice in certain kinds of Egyptian texts; is not a nod to women's status in Egypt or a reverence for motherhood but a purely practical matter. The identity of a person's biological mother was always certain, whereas the identity of the biological father might be in some doubt (note the later period documents in which children's fathers are identified as "Buirrekhirenef," literally "I don't know his name").[58] Djehutymose seems rather more confident of his father's identity, of course, but where there is room for one name only, Tareru's name is used more frequently (fig. 157). Thus covered in marks of identity, Djehutymose was sealed in this protective coffin and placed in his family tomb.

From Edfu to Ann Arbor: A Dispersal and a Reunion

After his funeral was over, Djehutymose lay buried in his family tomb, awaiting eternity, but what ultimately happened was far beyond anything he could have imagined. Whatever the fate of his spiritual components, Djehutymose's hopes for his physical remains did not ultimately go according to plan. The Djehutymose family burial at the cemetery at Nag el-Hassiya would have been opened repeatedly to accept new family burials, at least until the tomb was full. But the family was disturbed for other reasons at least once, possibly more. Although the shift in burial practice that led to fewer valuables in elite burials had removed some incentives for grave robbers, graves were still robbed in ancient times. Enough gold and precious stones were used in jewelry and amulets for elite mummies to make their burials attractive to ancient robbers. The heads and necks of mummies were often specifically targeted, leaving behind headless or heavily damaged mummies, and coffins were often damaged in the process of getting inside them (fig. 158). The damage sustained by Djehutymose's coffin might suggest an ancient robbery.

Fig. 158. View of child mummy in fig. 159 showing jaw dislocated by grave robbers.

Another ancient danger would have been intrusive burials. Long after family tombs were closed to further occupants, they were often re-opened in later periods for additional burials unrelated to the original tomb occupants. Sometimes, in this process, the contents of the older burials would be shoved aside, if not thrown out of the tomb altogether (one suspects that a fair amount of pilfering from the original burials went on when tombs were opened for intrusive burials as well). Djehutymose's coffin may have been damaged in the course of such intrusive burials being added to his family tomb; intrusive burials were particularly common in the Ptolemaic and earlier Roman Periods (c. 300 BC–AD 200). As traditional Egyptian burial practices began to decrease in the later Roman Period (third–fourth centuries AD), partly from the decline in importance of indigenous religion and partly from the growth and ultimate dominance of Christianity in Egypt, older burials suffered new disruptions. Christian monks began to inhabit ancient tombs as part of their ascetic, solitary monastic practice, and they did not particularly respect the wishes of the tombs' original occupants. Many tombs would have been cleared of their contents by monks looking for cells, although the more intrepid monks would live among the tombs' original occupants as a form of mortification or a reminder of mortality. The Coptic *Life* of the 7th-century AD bishop Pisentius of Coptos gives an extraordinary account of the finding of a mummy in a Theban tomb: the hagiographer describes Pisentius' revival of the mummy so that it can give an account of the torments of Hell.[59] (The Coptic word used for "Hell" is "Amenti," directly derived from the earlier Egyptian Amentet—the "West" to which all Egyptians aspired—thus giving an idea of the Egyptian Christians' feelings about the efficacy of earlier funerary beliefs.) Although monks continued to live in tombs for centuries after Pisentius' time, the Arab Conquest of Egypt in AD 639–642 and the subsequent growth and dominance of Islam in Egypt eventually curtailed this practice.

It is unknown whether Djehutymose's family tomb was used for a monastic cell, but even if so, such reuse would not have persisted indefinitely, and it is likely that the tomb was left more or less undisturbed in the centuries following the Arab Conquest. Only when European travelers started coming to Egypt in increasing numbers in the 17th, 18th, and especially 19th century did the pharaonic tombs become a renewed focus of interest. The growing interest in ancient Egypt among Europeans led to an increased demand for Egyptian antiquities, which led to the ever-increasing robbing of tombs. The beginnings of archaeological excavation in Egypt in the 19th century at least led to the recording of the contexts of some finds and the preservation of some groups of related material, but the looting of sites continued. Although attempts were made at regulating excavation of sites and the antiquities trade, the lack of means of enforcement in Egypt's subject, colonial status kept them from being effective. The development of scientific archaeology in Egypt, pioneered by Sir William Flinders Petrie beginning in the late 19th century, and the strengthening of antiquities laws in the early 20th century, helped record and control the finding of artifacts in their contexts, but the efficacy of both varied widely.

Such is the context of the modern discovery of Djehutymose's coffin. Finds from the Nag el-Hassiya cemetery began appearing on the antiquities market in the late 19th century, and there were formal excavations at the site in the late 19th and early 20th centuries. A large group of coffins is known to have come from the site in the mid-1880s,[60] while archaeologist John Garstang recorded an intact Ptolemaic tomb group found at Nag el-Hassiya in 1905 (now in Liverpool).[61] The precise circumstances under which Djehutymose's family tomb was discovered are not known, whether formal (if undocumented or unpublished) excavation or illegal looting. What is certain is that at some point, either in ancient or modern times, Djehutymose's coffin was separated from his mummy (the fate of which is unknown) and also from the Ptah-Sokar-Osiris figures from his family tomb, as well as from any other related artifacts and material from other burials in the tomb that may have survived. The Djehutymose coffin is first known in modern times as being in the collection of Albert M. Todd (1850–1931) (fig. 159). Mr. Todd was a U.S. politician and businessman, known as the "Peppermint King" for his role in developing processes for the manufacture and grading of mint flavorings and oils, based in Kalamazoo, Michigan. Although Mr. Todd purchased some of his Egyptian antiquities from the well-known Amherst collection, Djehutymose's coffin does not seem to come from this source, and it is unclear whether Todd purchased it in Egypt or elsewhere.[62]

Regardless of exactly when and where Djehutymose's coffin was purchased, we know that it must have taken at least one long boat voyage across the Atlantic before 1906—at that time, the only practical way to ship such an object overseas. The coffin would have been packed in a wooden crate, possibly with other antiquities, and taken a trip of several

Fig. 159. Albert M. Todd (photo courtesy of Chemical Heritage Foundation Collections).

Fig. 160. Child mummy, Ptolemaic Period, 332–30 BC, human remains, cloth, plaster, paint, gilding (KM 1989.3.3).

Fig. 161. Mummy mask, Ptolemaic Period, 332–30 BC, cloth, plaster, paint, gilding (KM 1989.3.2).

days to reach the U.S. safely. In 1906 Djehutymose's coffin, along with a few other objects (figs. 160–161), was presented by Mr. Todd to the University of Michigan, and in 1931 the coffin became part of the collection of the relatively new Museum of Classical Archaeology. This museum was, at the time, as much a theoretical construct as an active, working museum: most of its activities and attentions were taken up by material coming in from the University of Michigan's excavations at Hellenistic and Roman Period sites throughout the Mediterranean world. In particular, the Michigan excavations at Karanis in the Egyptian Fayum were yielding prodigious amounts of material (more than 45,000 objects had been sent back to Ann Arbor by the end of the project in 1935), and the museum's primary focus was dealing with these materials and housing them in the building leased for this purpose beginning in 1928 (and ultimately purchased by the university in 1937). Given this situation, the Djehutymose coffin was placed on long-term loan with the Kalamazoo Public Museum, along with a number of other Egyptian objects. The location was significant in that it was a museum in Mr. Todd's own town and one to which he had presented another mummy case, a Saite coffin from Qubbet el-Hawa that he had acquired from the sale of the collection of Lord Amherst of Hackney in 1921.[63] Indeed, Todd's donations of antiquities and European art had helped establish the Kalamazoo Public Museum in 1927.[64] Djehutymose's coffin quickly became an integral and beloved part of the Kalamazoo Public Museum display, alongside a number of other coffins (fig. 162).

Meanwhile, another part of Djehutymose's burial reached Ann Arbor by a very different route. In 1935, the University of Michigan Expedition to Egypt was winding up its archaeological projects there—completing the 11-year Karanis excavation as well as a quick month at the western Delta site of Kom Abou Billou, the Graeco-Roman cemetery of Terenouthis. As there were no plans to return to Egypt in the foreseeable future, the Michigan group took advantage of their final months in Egypt to purchase additional material for the burgeoning Museum of Archaeology collection. (It is important to remember that in 1935 the sale of antiquities in Egypt was still legal and their export permitted, unlike the situation today.) Although some of the acquisitions were from the well-known antiquities dealer Phocion Tano, the bulk of material was acquired from the Egyptian Department of Antiquities itself. From this source, the University of Michigan acquired a group of later period funerary objects. Among these objects were four

Fig. 162. The Djehutymose coffin (*second from left*) on display in the Kalamazoo Public Museum, 1930s (photo from the collection of the Kalamazoo Valley Museum).

Ptah-Sokar-Osiris figures, two of which belonged to Djehutymose and his brother, and a third that may have belonged to his mother, along with some painted wooden falcons that likely came from these figures' original bases. The connection between the figures and the coffin had not yet been made, however, and they appear to have been chosen simply as examples of types of objects not represented in the University of Michigan collections. These purchases were apparently shipped back to Michigan along with the final crates of excavated material from Karanis and Terenouthis.

World War II put an end to Michigan's field activities for a while, and in Ann Arbor attention turned toward the Museum of Archaeology and its contents. Given the strong Graeco-Roman Period emphasis of the museum's collection, little work was done on the dynastic Egyptian material beyond basic cataloguing and storage, and Djehutymose's coffin was left at the Kalamazoo Public Museum. As the Ann Arbor museum's profile increased, both as a local attraction and also as a University of Michigan resource, interest increased in its collections as well, and more of the earlier Egyptian material was put on display. In 1953, the museum was renamed after its founder Francis W. Kelsey as the Kelsey Museum of Archaeology. Interest in the museum's holdings of Egyptian material continued to grow, and its collection of dynastic Egyptian artifacts was substantially increased by the acquisition of the Bay View Collection in 1971: this material was originally acquired in Egypt in the late 19th century for a small, biblically oriented museum in Bay View, Michigan. (Figs. 9–12, 37, 64, 76, 88, 97, 106, 113, 127, 129, 135–136, and 142 show objects from the Bay View Collection.) The Kelsey Museum also had long-term loans of Egyptian objects to supplement its collections, including loans from the Metropolitan Museum of Art in New York and the private loan of an extensive illustrated Book of the Dead papyrus.[65] The donation of the Egyptian collection of Dr. Samuel A. Goudsmit, retired University of Michigan professor, increased the Kelsey Museum's holdings further with the addition of a number of papyri and other inscribed objects, including the Montuemhat funerary cone and papyrus fragment of Khamhor illustrated above. (Figs. 2–3, 39, 77, 126, 128, 145, and 151 illustrate objects from the Goudsmit Collection.)[66]

Djehutymose in the Kelsey Museum of Archaeology

In the late 1980s, increasing interest in the Kelsey Museum's Dynastic Period Egyptian material led to new interest in the Djehutymose coffin. The museum was on the verge of constructing a new state-of-the-art conservation facility, and this was seen as a perfect opportunity to bring the Djehutymose coffin back to Ann Arbor. The formalities for the return of the coffin were completed in 1989, and the coffin itself arrived at the Kelsey in 1990. Almost immediately, the nearly 100,000 other objects in the Kelsey Museum had to go into storage in preparation for the construction of its new Sensitive Artifact Facility and Environment (SAFE), funded by Kelsey Museum supporters Eugene and Emily Grant, with help from the National Endowment for the Humanities Heritage Preservation Program and a wide range of Kelsey supporters and friends. Although stored objects were deliberately kept inaccessible during this project to ensure their stability, one major exception was made for University of Chicago Egyptology student Jonathan Elias, who was permitted to examine Djehutymose's coffin in storage for its first, in-depth scholarly treatment in his 1993 doctoral dissertation on post-New Kingdom coffin inscriptions. Since display of the coffin was to be a priority once the museum reopened, conservator Geoff Brown undertook the delicate work, in a project funded by Kelsey Museum supporters Linda and Todd Herrick.

The reopening of the Kelsey Museum in the fall of 1994 coincided with the arrival of two new staff members who would soon become very familiar with Djehutymose's coffin, Egyptologists Janet Richards and Terry Wilfong. They were (initially) temporary employees charged with the task of curating a special exhibition to celebrate the new SAFE facility and showcase the newly restored Djehutymose coffin. This 1995 exhibition, our first at the Kelsey Museum, was called "Preserving Eternity," and it drew parallels between modern conservation approaches and ancient Egyptian intentions of preservation. Djehutymose's coffin formed the centerpiece for the exhibition, and its conservation was documented for the catalogue.[67] For the exhibition, the coffin lid and base were displayed horizontally in separate cases (fig. 163). The two parts of the coffin were gently elevated above mirrors, allowing the viewer to see the image of the goddess Nut under the lid and the elaborate Djed pillar on the bottom of the base—images that would normally not have been visible.

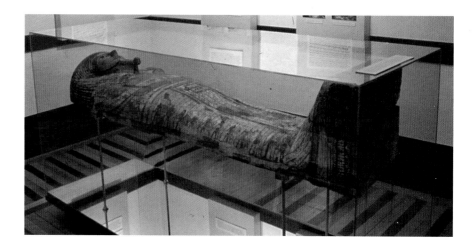

The "Preserving Eternity" exhibition was also intended to show the results of a survey of the Kelsey Museum Egyptian collection undertaken by Richards and Wilfong, which highlighted a number of significant Egyptian objects that were unpublished and had not previously been displayed. The research on these objects revealed many new and surprising things about the collection. But perhaps the greatest surprise was Wilfong's discovery of the connection between the Djehutymose coffin and the three Djehutymose family Ptah-Sokar-Osiris statues. The combination of the inscriptional and stylistic evidence for connections between the pieces was conclusive, and the coincidental reunion of these pieces from a family burial near Edfu in a museum in Ann Arbor, Michigan, was featured in the resulting exhibition and catalogue.[68]

After the closing of "Preserving Eternity," the Djehutymose coffin and related Ptah-Sokar-Osiris figures remained on display in their new home, what was once referred to as the "Fireplace Gallery" in the old Kelsey Museum building. The Djehutymose coffin quickly became one of the most popular objects on display, an obligatory stop for all school and university groups touring the museum. As Richards and Wilfong became curators and faculty members at the university, the Djehutymose coffin began to inform their teaching, and their students often got to know it well. It was featured in survey courses and graduate seminars on Egyptian archaeology, history, and religion. The few students who survived the first two terms of Egyptian language instruction also got to know Djehutymose *very* well in the third term, when copying, translating, and understanding the text of the inside of the coffin base regularly formed the final class project.

The original Kelsey Museum building where Djehutymose was initially displayed is a beautiful example of the late 19th-century Richardsonian Romanesque architecture that characterizes a number of the older buildings in Ann Arbor. Originally known as Newberry Hall, the building was constructed in 1888–1891 as the home for the Student Christian Association, which function it served until acquired by the University of Michigan for its archaeology museum.[69] But the building was never intended as a museum: its rooms were not constructed as museum galleries and were never particularly suited for the display of sensitive ancient organic materials, such as the wood out of which Djehutymose's coffin was made. The goal of the museum had long been a project to build a fully climate-controlled display wing onto the existing, historic Kelsey Museum building. Thanks to the extraordinary generosity of Edwin and Mary Meader, this vision became a reality. In 2006, ground was broken on what would become the William E. Upjohn Exhibit Wing of the Kelsey Museum of Archaeology, a state of the art facility for the display and storage of artifacts that would more than quadruple existing display areas with full climate control and an expanded artifact storage facility. Again Djehutymose went back into storage, as the Kelsey Museum closed for several years' worth of renovation and construction.

For the new installation, curator Janet Richards decided that the Djehutymose coffin needed a new display strategy. Although the use of mirrors in the old installation allowed viewers to glimpse the painting of the goddess Nut on the inside of the coffin lid, it was impossible to see the whole figure or get a good idea of its overall impact. Improving the visibility of the interior of the coffin, and especially the image of the goddess Nut, shaped the new concept for the display of the coffin—the idea that all surfaces would be visible. There was also the idea that, by raising to prominence the faces of the images of goddesses Nut and Amentet, the new display of the coffin would increase the visibility of female faces in the gallery, to subtly underline the relatively high position that women held in Egyptian society. Ultimately, curator Richards decided that the coffin should be displayed upright, and this was in keeping with the Egyptian practice of standing coffins on end for the burial ceremonies: indeed Djehutymose's coffin was designed with a square base at the foot just for this purpose.

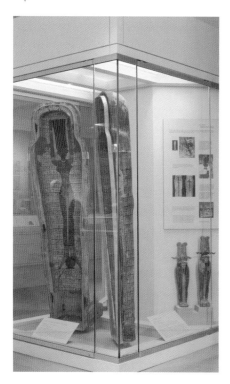

Fig. 164. The Djehutymose coffin as installed in 2009 in the Kelsey Museum's William E. Upjohn Exhibit Wing (photo Sebastián Encina).

Egyptian coffins were often displayed upright in museums in the past (this is how the Djehutymose coffin was displayed in Kalamazoo), but concerns about conservation and stress on ancient wood have led modern museums to tend to display such coffins horizontally. So the first step in devising a mount for a new, upright display of the Djehutymose coffin was to address these real conservation concerns. Curator Richards, preparator Scott Meier and conservators Suzanne Davis and Claudia Chemello worked with mount makers from Multiform Studios to create a framework that would allow the Djehutymose coffin to stand upright but protect its fragile wood and painted surfaces from stress and damage. In the meantime, the conservators undertook a thorough review of the condition of the coffin and carried out new treatments to stabilize the coffin for display. Before the Djehutymose coffin was put back on display, University Library photographer Randal Stegmeyer made a complete set of new photographs (which have been used throughout this book). The new installation of the Djehutymose coffin and the Ptah-Sokar-Osiris figures from the Djehutymose family burial was a prominent feature of the opening of the new display wing of the Kelsey Museum in 2009 (fig. 164).

The Kelsey Museum's current installation of the Djehutymose coffin in the Upjohn Exhibit Wing combines old and new display strategies for mummy cases into a unique visual experience for the visitor. Nearly all surfaces of the coffin are visible and accessible; the coffin is displayed alongside the related Ptah-Sokar-Osiris figures and is accompanied by extensive didactic material designed to explain the coffin and place it in its wider context. The surrounding cases in the gallery, with their complement of Egyptian funerary artifacts and images, many of which are illustrated in the preceding pages, mirror, echo, and amplify the dramatic view of Djehutymose's coffin. By standing in front of the coffin as it is displayed now, the viewer not only gets to see the dramatic paintings of the interior of the coffin but also experiences the coffin much as Djehutymose himself might have just before it was closed.

The Djehutymose Coffin in the 21st Century

Since its reinstallation in the Kelsey Museum William E. Upjohn Exhibit Wing, the Djehutymose coffin has attracted a great deal of attention. It is a magnet for visitors, and it is not unusual to see groups of children and adults clustered around it. The coffin is such a valuable tool for teaching about ancient Egypt that it features prominently in many courses at the University of Michigan, as well as local K–12 classes. The combination of texts and images seen on the coffin is a compelling juxtaposition, and the Djehutymose coffin has featured in numerous university campaigns, including the promotional materials for the University of Michigan College of Literature, Science, and the Arts Theme Semesters on "Meaningful Objects: Museums in the Academy" and "Language: The Human Quintessence." Thus, gods and goddesses from Djehutymose's coffin looked on from banners across the university campus, and one enterprising animator even took them for a walk around campus (fig. 165).[70]

Fig. 165. Still from video for the University of Michigan College of Literature, Science, and the Arts "Language" Theme Semester (video and concept by Hans Anderson, using photograph by Randal Stegmeyer).

Not surprisingly, the Djehutymose coffin features prominently in Kelsey Museum public programming and outreach as well. One of the most popular recurring events at the Kelsey Museum is the regular Egyptian-themed "Family Day," a workshop for children where they get to make their own mummies and related funerary equipment while learning about the processes and ideas behind the making of mummies. These hands-on workshops are the brainchild of former Kelsey Museum Associate Director Lauren Talalay and Todd Gerring, the Kelsey Museum's Community Outreach Supervisor, whose clever use of humble materials (off-brand dolls, candies, shoeboxes, etc.) to make ancient Egyptian artifacts has made this event so popular that it now has a waiting list.[71] The preparations are intensive: plastic dolls have their body cavities filled with gummi worms, jellybeans, and other edibles to simulate internal organs that the children will remove and place in canopic jars (made of appropriately decorated film canisters) to learn about the embalming process (fig. 166). The participants customize shoebox coffins with a template patterned after the Djehutymose coffin, wrap their eviscerated dolls in bandages, and create their own mummies, learning about life and death in ancient Egypt while having fun.

Fig. 166. Mummy making kit for Kelsey Museum "Family Day" (photo author).

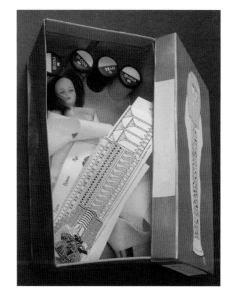

The Djehutymose coffin is a highly visible presence in the museum and, as such, often attracts sketchers and other artists—from full-fledged art classes to casual hobbyists, many of whom take away their own highly

Fig. 167. John Kannenberg, "Subset 2: Two Hours of Infinity: Shen," 2012, charcoal on paper with fishing line, gravity, time, and sound, 30" x 22" (private collection).

Fig. 168. John Kannenberg, "An Hour of Infinity" performance: artist Charlie Michaels drawing near the Djehutymose coffin (Kelsey Museum of Archaeology, 23 March 2012; photo Sebastián Encina).

individual interpretations of Djehutymose in their artwork. Since the opening of the Kelsey Museum's new wing, local artists have "rediscovered" the Kelsey, and in particular students and faculty of the university's School of Art and Design have found a source of inspiration in the Kelsey and also, increasingly, a welcoming venue for their work. One recent project drew direct inspiration from Djehutymose and even surrounded the coffin with artistic practice and performance. In 2011, artist John Kannenberg began a drawing project, including a series of drawings of shen signs like the one on Djehutymose's coffin (fig. 167).[72] These drawings were part of a larger project, "Hours of Infinity," that used drawing, sound, and live performance to examine themes of eternity and infinity in the context of the Kelsey Museum. This project culminated in "An Hour of Infinity" performed at the Kelsey Museum on 23 March 2012 (fig. 168), an installation and performance piece. For one hour, Djehutymose serenely presided in the midst of a surround-sound composition based on the noises of the gallery floor in the old building, while musicians played and artists drew endless iterations on the symbols of infinity under the direction of Kannenberg as visitors circulated throughout the galleries. Ancient and contemporary art came together in this unique event.[73]

It is clear that the coffin has acquired its own personality as "Djehutymose": the lack of a mummy has not prevented Kelsey visitors and fans from personifying the coffin as the person that it was made for, and Djehutymose has become an important part of the local Kelsey Museum community. But the Djehutymose coffin is known to a wider audience well beyond Ann Arbor, thanks to Djehutymose's active presence on social media. Djehutymose maintains a lively Facebook page,[74] on which he discusses himself, other Kelsey Museum objects, and material in other museum collections, and where he promotes Kelsey Museum events. Djehutymose's online reach is further expanded by his active embrace of Twitter,[75] and his tweets give him a somewhat more immediate platform for publicizing the Kelsey Museum. Of course, Djehutymose has an amanuensis for his communications, and this is Kelsey Museum docent Marlene Goldsmith, a retired PR executive who has thrown herself into Djehutymose's online activities with great enthusiasm and inventiveness. Her Djehutymose postings and tweets reflect careful thought and planning, and Marlene works in consultation with the Kelsey Museum's Egyptological curators in shaping Djehutymose's online persona and specific comments. As of the end of

169   170

2012, the Djehutymose coffin had 1,490 Facebook friends and 1,157 followers on Twitter, many of whom are very active in Djehutymose's behalf (figs. 169–170).

Djehutymose is not a passive online presence but gets his followers and friends involved, posing questions and initiating dialogues with other museums and their mummies. Perhaps the most pressing issue that Djehutymose has been pursuing is deeply personal: attempting to find his missing mummy, separated from its coffin at some point before 1931. Although to date the mummy has not been found, in the process Djehutymose has made many new friends, fans, and followers and has helped raise interest in the idea of reuniting mummies with their coffins in other collections.

Fig. 169. Djehutymose on Facebook, 7 February 2013.

Fig. 170. Djehutymose on Twitter, 7 February 2013.

Conclusion

Djehutymose's active 21st-century "afterlife" attests to the enduring popularity of ancient Egypt and the direct and personal connections that people of our time feel to the ancient Egyptians. The Djehutymose coffin serves as an intermediary between past and present in the Kelsey Museum and beyond. Not only can we understand the coffin for what it is—a museum artifact with a complex history—but we can also use it to get to know an ancient Egyptian individual, his family, and his world.

Notes

1. For standard histories of the Saite Period, see James 1991 and Lloyd 2000. Note that most kings of this period tend to be known in the scholarly literature by the Greek renderings of their names, so both Egyptian and Greek names are given below.

2. For the Montuemhat funerary cones, see Richards and Wilfong 1995, 47–48; the Khamhor papyrus fragment is published in Wilfong 2012.

3. For the date, see Elias 1993, 842–844; Elias allows that the possible dates for Djehutymose's coffin could extend into the reign of Ahmose II (Amasis), 570–526 BC, but sees the earlier dates as more likely.

4. *Ḏḥwtj.ms(.w)*, substantive + stative (Allen 2010, §17.9 at 212). Since Egyptian does not indicate vowels and the values of certain consonants shift over time, modern phonetic renderings of Egyptian names are usually approximate and can vary widely. Thus this name is variously given as Djehutymose or Djheutymose, but also as Thutmosis and Thutmose (most often for the kings bearing this name). In this book, we use Djehutymose for our coffin owner and Thutmose for the 18th Dynasty king.

5. For a useful guide to the Ptolemaic temple at Edfu, see Kurth 2004.

6. The description of the temple ritual at Edfu is drawn largely from Meeks and Favard-Meeks 1996.

7. See Kurth 1994, 147–150 for references and a German translation of these texts.

8. For animal mummies and their cults in general, see Ikram 2004.

9. See Robins 1993 for the status and roles of women in ancient Egypt in general, and 99–101 for this title in particular.

10. Donker van Heel 2012 provides a fascinating look at the business activities of a family of funerary priests in the later Saite Period.

11. For a translation of the "classic" harper's song, see Simpson 2003, 332–333 and for references to these and other harper's songs, 558–559. See also the Greek author Herodotus (Book II.78; standard text and translation in the Loeb edition: 364–365).

12. For the demographic information available from Roman Egypt and its interpretation, see Bagnall and Frier 1994, especially 91–110 for information relevant to the present discussion.

13. See Zakrezewski 2003, especially the summary at 224. Note that these totals are ±4–5 cm, but even with these variations, Djehutymose would still come close to an average or slightly taller height.

14. For the embalming process, see Taylor 2001, 46–91.

15. Taylor 2001, 56.

16. Egyptian artists, as a rule, did not sign their work, so we do not know the name

of the painter of Djehutymose's coffin. Given the social conventions of the time in ancient Egypt, it is practically certain that the artist was a man, hence the references to him as such below.

17. In coffins of this period, this particular inscription of five lines above the legs was usually done in color, sometimes even inlaid. Elias 1993, 835, n. 170 describes in detail the technique of the painting of this inscription.

18. Taylor 2001, 57.

19. For bead nets in general, see Aston 2009, 290–293. See Bosse-Griffiths 1978, 105 for the burial of Harsiese, a priest of Horus of Edfu and near contemporary of Djehutymose, with a bead net covered with cartonnage, reference from Aston 2009, 290.

20. For the dual meaning of these embalming scenes, see Corcoran 1995, 57–58; Corcoran and Svoboda 2012, 74–75 further develops this reading of such scenes as a reflection of the Egyptian understandings of time as both cyclical and linear.

21. Taylor 2001 18–23.

22. For the opening of the mouth for speech, see, for example, Book of the Dead, chapters 23–25 (Allen 1960, 108–110), and note the later period books for opening the mouth for breathing, Smith 2009, 349–387.

23. Munro 1973, 68–70.

24. Aston 2009 surveys the contents of known burial assemblages in the period just before Djehutymose's time and is a useful guide to the possible contents of Djehutymose's burial.

25. Gray and Slow 1968, 5.

26. Quirke 1993, 19–21.

27. Munro 1973, 68–70 and de Meulenaere 1969.

28. Gray and Slow 1968, 41–42.

29. For Ptah-Sokar-Osiris figures, their decoration, texts, and adjuncts, see Raven 1978–1979. I owe a great debt of thanks to Maarten Raven for his advice and opinions on the Kelsey figures.

30. See Raven 1978–1979, 286–287 for grain mummies specific to Ptah-Sokar-Osiris figures and Raven 1982 for grain mummies in general. Note that these are frequently referred to as "corn mummies" in the literature, but this reflects the English usage of "corn" as a generic term for cereal grains versus the American usage of "corn" for maize, a crop indigenous to the New World and not found in ancient Egypt.

31. See Gray and Slow 1968, 4–5 for these later mummies.

32. Reeves 1990, 105–106.

33. For Egyptian gods in general, Wilkinson 2003 is an excellent reference; for much more detailed information and references, the massive Leitz 2002 is essential.

34. See Elias 1993, 805–806 for a discussion of the Nut images on later period coffins, but note that table 76 on p. 824 mistakenly characterizes the representation of Nut on Djehutymose's coffin as nude.
35. For this explanation, see Quack 2004.
36. For this god, see Leitz 2002, V:262–263.
37. For these gods, see Leitz 2002: Hekamaitef, V:27–28, Kherybakef, VI:36–37, and Iryrenefdjesef, I:471–472.
38. See Ritner 2008, 57–67 for the magic of encircling.
39. "Thoth" is the Greek rendering of the Egyptian name we are rendering "Djehuty"; the Greek name is so much more common in the literature than the Egyptian for this god that we use "Thoth" here to refer to the god.
40. Corcoran and Svoboda 2010, 23–24.
41. See, for example, Cairo Museum CGC 41045 and 41059 (Gauthier 1913, plates 7 and 25 respectively).
42. See Kannenberg 2012 and discussion below on page 100.
43. See Andrews 1994, 96.
44. See Wilkinson 1992, 171 for a discussion of the use of this symbol.
45. The textual program of later period coffins like Djehutymose's has been the object of in-depth study by Egyptologists Jonathan Elias and, more recently, Martin von Falck, and the discussion and translations that follow draw heavily on the work of these two scholars: Elias 1993 and Falck 2001.
46. Raven 1981, 16–17 and Elias 1993, 834.
47. On the use of threats in Egyptian magic, see Ritner 2008, 5–6, 21–22.
48. Elias 1993, 557–584, which collects together the parallels, is essential for understanding the heavily abbreviated versions of these texts on Djehutymose's coffin.
49. The name of the god Khepri and the verb "to come into being" are written with the same hieroglyph—plays on words and gods' names are common in Egyptian religious texts.
50. Variants have "the bones of Osiris" instead of "beauty": Elias 1993, 582–583.
51. This text is derived from the Eye of Horus text 2 often found on later coffins: Elias 1993, 590.
52. Allen 1960, 69–70.
53. For the identification and location of ancient Egyptian places in general, see Baines and Malek 2000.
54. The texts translated here are a combination of Elias' "Recombined Spells" 1.2 and 1.1, Elias' Nut texts 13D.4 and 13D.5 and Book of the Dead, chapter 169. A short section of text in the middle remains unidentified and is left untranslated for now.
55. For this rendering and a grammatical analysis and discussion of the formula, see Allen 2010, §24.10 at 365–367.

56. Taylor 2001, 58–59.

57. For the concept of a "beautiful burial," albeit somewhat after Djehutymose's time, see Riggs 2005, 2.

58. For these documents, with references, see De Pauw 1997, 136–137.

59. For an accessible English translation of this story, see Lewis and Burstein 2001, 101–110.

60. Elias 1993, 552.

61. Gray and Slow 1968, 41–42.

62. For more information about Albert M. Todd, see http://www.kpl.gov/local-history/biographies/albert-todd.aspx. For an early reference to the Djehutymose coffin at the University of Michigan, see D'Ooge 1906.

63. Elias 1996, especially 105 and n. 2.

64. For Todd's collection, see http://kvm.kvcc.edu/localhistory/thecollection/am-todd/.

65. The lender, Dr. O. O. Fisher of Detroit, eventually retrieved his papyrus, but he donated to the Kelsey Museum his sumptuous copy of the Napoleonic *Description de l'Égypte* (Paris: Imprimerie Impériale, 1809–1822), now Kelsey Museum 2003.4.1a–w, perhaps as consolation for the withdrawal of his papyrus.

66. See Root 1981 for the Goudsmit Collection.

67. Hogg 1995, and see also Richards and Wilfong 1995, 50–51.

68. Wilfong 1995; note that the possible Ptah-Sokar-Osiris figure of Djehutymose's mother had not been identified as such when this article was written.

69. http://www.lsa.umich.edu/kelsey/aboutus/history.

70. http://www.lsa.umich.edu/museumstheme/ and http://language.lsa.umich.edu/.

71. http://www.lsa.umich.edu/kelsey/publicprograms/familydays.

72. Kannenberg 2012.

73. "Hours of Infinity" video at http://vimeo.com/40366610 and see also http://www.johnkannenberg.com/.

74. Djehutymose's Facebook account is at: http://www.facebook.com/Djehutymose.

75. Djehutymose on Twitter: https://twitter.com/@Djehutymose.

Suggested Reading

The notes below provide references for specific points in the text, but more general references inform this work throughout and may be of interest for further reading and research. Many of the books cited below are used as textbooks or references in my introductory survey courses on Egyptian religion and history and are thus classroom-tested by my students.

Little has been published specifically on the Djehutymose coffin. Elias 1993 was the first scholarly work on the coffin's texts and images, as part of a larger survey of later period coffins. The coffin was also featured in the exhibition catalogue Richards and Wilfong 1995. Since then, Falck 2001 made some note of Djehutymose's coffin from the information in Elias, but no further work on the coffin has appeared in print.

In recent years, scholars have been using mummies and their coffins and other funerary equipment as a means of getting to know individual Egyptians and their worlds: Corcoran and Svoboda 2010 and Taylor 1995 and 2011 are fascinating reading and extremely informative.

Perhaps the best general reference to Egyptian funerary beliefs and practices is Taylor 2001. For Egyptian religion in general, Teeter 2011 and Shafer 1991 provide useful surveys, while Meeks and Favard-Meeks 1996 is a fascinating study of temple cult in the later period, and Wilkinson 2000 is a useful overview of ancient temples throughout Egypt. Wilkinson 2003 provides a comprehensive survey of the gods and goddesses of ancient Egypt. For reading the symbolism of Egyptian images and texts, Wilkinson 1992 and 1994 are extremely informative. Egyptian history is surveyed in Shaw 2000, and standard accounts of the Saite Period can be found in James 1991 and Lloyd 2000. For the lives of the priestly elites in the later periods, the exhibition catalogue Teeter and Johnson 2009 is a useful guide.

Bibliography

Allen, J. P. 2010. *Middle Egyptian: An Introduction to the Language and Culture of Hieroglyphs.* 2nd edition. Cambridge: Cambridge University Press.

Allen, T. G. 1960. *The Egyptian Book of the Dead: Documents in the Oriental Institute Museum, University of Chicago.* Oriental Institute Publications 82. Chicago: University of Chicago Press.

Andrews, C. 1994. *Amulets of Ancient Egypt.* London: British Museum Press.

Aston, D. A. 2009. *Burial Assemblages of Dynasty 21–25: Chronology, Typology, Developments.* Contributions to the Chronology of the Eastern Mediterranean 21. Vienna: Verlag der Österreichischen Akademie der Wissenschaften.

Bagnall, R. S. and B. W. Frier. 1994. *The Demography of Roman Egypt.* Cambridge Studies in Population, Economy and Society in Past Time 23. Cambridge: Cambridge University Press.

Baines, J. and J. Malek. 2000. *Cultural Atlas of Ancient Egypt.* New York: Checkmark.

Bosse-Griffiths, K. 1978. "Some Egyptian Bead-Work Faces in the Wellcome Collection at University College, Swansea." *Journal of Egyptian Archaeology* 64: 99–106.

Corcoran, L. H. 1995. *Portrait Mummies from Roman Egypt.* Studies in Ancient Oriental Civilization 56. Chicago: Oriental Institute Press.

Corcoran, L. H and M. Svoboda. 2010. *Herakleides: A Portrait Mummy from Roman Egypt.* Los Angeles: J. Paul Getty Museum.

de Meulenaere, H. 1969. "Les stèles de Nag el-Hassaïa." *Mitteilungen des deutschen archäologischen Instituts Abteilung Kairo* 25: 90–97.

De Pauw, M. 1997. *A Companion to Demotic Studies.* Papyrologica Bruxellensia 28. Brussels: Fondation Égyptologique Reine Élisabeth.

Donker van Heel, K. 2012. *Djekhy & Son: Doing Business in Ancient Egypt.* Cairo: American University in Cairo Press.

D'Ooge, M. L. 1906. *Catalogue of the Gallery of Art and Archaeology in the University of Michigan.* Ann Arbor: University of Michigan.

Elias, J. 1993. "Coffin Inscription in Egypt after the New Kingdom: A Study of Text Production and Use in Elite Mortuary Preparation." Ph.D. dissertation, University of Chicago.

———. 1996. "Regional Indicia on a Saite Coffin from Qubbet el-Hawa." *Journal of the American Research Center in Egypt* 33: 105–122.

Falck, M. v. 2001. "Textgeschichtliche Untersuchungen zu Götterreden und verwandten Texten auf ägyptischen Särgen und Sarkophagen von der 3. Zwischenzeit bis zur Ptolemäerzeit." Ph.D. dissertation, Westfälischen-Wilhelms Universität, Münster (Westf.).

Gauthier, H. 1913. *Cercueils anthropoïdes des prêtres de Montou: Catalogue générale des antiquités égyptiennes du Musée du Caire, Nos. 41042–41072.* Cairo: Imprimerie de l'Institut Français d'Archéologie Orientale.

Gray, P. H. K. and D. Slow. 1968. "Egyptian Mummies in the City of Liverpool Museums." *Liverpool Bulletin: Libraries, Museums and Arts Committee* 15: 1–76.

Hogg, Alan J. 1995. "Conserving the Coffin of Djheutymose." In Richards and Wilfong, 1995, 53–55.

Ikram, S., ed. 2004. *Divine Creatures: Animal Mummies in Ancient Egypt.* Cairo: American University in Cairo Press.

James, T. G. H. 1991. "Egypt: The Twenty-Fifth and Twenty-Sixth Dynasties." In *Cambridge Ancient History, Second Edition, Volume Three, Part Two.* Cambridge: Cambridge University Press. Pp. 677–747, 860–867.

Kannenberg, J. 2012. *Hours of Infinity: Recording the Imperfect Eternal.* Kelsey Museum Publication 8. Ann Arbor: Kelsey Museum of Archaeology.

Kurth, D. 1994. *Treffpunkt der Götter: Inschriften aus dem Tempel des Horus von Edfu.* Zürich/Munich: Artemis Verlag.

———. 2004. *The Temple of Edfu: A Guide by an Ancient Egyptian Priest.* Cairo: American University in Cairo Press.

Leitz, C. 2002. *Lexikon der ägyptischen Götter und Götterbezeichnungen.* 8 volumes. Orientalia Lovanensia Analecta 110–116, 129. Leuven: Peeters.

Lewis, B. and S. Burstein, eds. 2001. *Land of the Enchanters: Egyptian Stories from the Earliest Times to the Present Day.* Princeton: Markus Weiner Publishers.

Lloyd, A. B. 2000. "The Late Period." In Shaw 2000, 369–394.

Meeks, D. and C. Favard-Meeks. 1996. *Daily Life of the Egyptian Gods.* Ithaca, NY: Cornell University Press.

Munro, P. 1973. *Die spätägyptischen Totenstelen.* Ägyptologische Forschungen 25. Gluckstadt: J. J. Augustin.

Quack, J. F. 2004. "Der pränatale Geschlechtsverkehr von Isis und Osiris sowie eine Notiz zum Alter des Osiris." *Studien zur altägyptischen Kultur* 32: 327–332.

Quirke, S. 1993. *Owners of Funerary Papyri in the British Museum.* British Museum Occasional Papers 92. London: British Museum.

Raven, M. 1978–1979. "Papyrus Sheaths and Ptah-Sokar-Osiris Statues." *Oudheidkundige Mededelingen* 59–60: 251–296.

———. 1981. "On Some Coffins of the Besenmut Family." *Oudheidkundige Mededelingen* 62: 7–21.

———. 1982. "Corn Mummies." *Oudheidkundige Mededelingen* 63:7–38.

Reeves, N. 1990. *The Complete Tutankhamun.* London: Thames & Hudson.

Richards, J. E. and T. G. Wilfong. 1995. *Preserving Eternity: Modern Goals, Ancient Intentions: Egyptian Funerary Artifacts in the Kelsey Museum of Archaeology.* Ann Arbor: Kelsey Museum of Archaeology.

Riggs, C. 2005. *The Beautiful Burial in Roman Egypt: Art, Identity and Funerary Religion*. Oxford Studies in Ancient Culture and Representation. Oxford: Oxford University Press.

Ritner, R. K. 2008. *The Mechanics of Ancient Egyptian Magical Practice*. Corrected 4th printing. Studies in Ancient Oriental Civilization 54. Chicago: Oriental Institute Press.

Robins, G. 1993. *Women in Ancient Egypt*. Cambridge, MA: Harvard University Press.

Root, M. C. 1981. *A Scientist Views the Past: The Samuel A. Goudsmit Collection of Egyptian Antiquities*. Ann Arbor: Kelsey Museum.

Shafer, B. E., ed. 1991. *Religion in Ancient Egypt: Gods, Myths and Personal Practice*. Ithaca, NY: Cornell University Press.

Shaw, I., ed. 2000. *The Oxford History of Ancient Egypt*. Oxford: Oxford University Press.

Simpson, W. K., ed. 2003. *The Literature of Ancient Egypt: An Anthology of Stories, Instructions, Stelae, Autobiographies and Poetry*. New Haven: Yale University Press.

Smith, M. 2009. *Traversing Eternity: Texts for the Afterlife from Ptolemaic and Roman Egypt*. Oxford: Oxford University Press.

Taylor, J. 1995. *Unwrapping a Mummy: The Life, Death and Embalming of Horemkenesi*. Egyptian Bookshelf. London: British Museum Press.

———. 2001. *Death and the Afterlife in Ancient Egypt*. London: British Museum Press.

———. 2011. *Mummy: The Inside Story*. London: British Museum Press.

Teeter, E. 2011. *Religion and Ritual in Ancient Egypt*. Cambridge: Cambridge University Press.

Teeter, E. and J. H. Johnson, eds. 2009. *The Life of Meresamun: A Temple Singer in Ancient Egypt*. Oriental Institute Museum Publications 29. Chicago: Oriental Institute Press.

Wilfong, T. G. 1995. "A Previously Unsuspected Connection." In Richards and Wilfong, 1995, 52.

———. 2012. "A Saite Book of the Dead Fragment in the Kelsey Museum of Archaeology." In *Papyrological Texts in Honor of Roger S. Bagnall*. Durham: American Society of Papyrologists. Pp. 325–330.

Wilkinson, R. H. 1992. *Reading Egyptian Art*. London: Thames and Hudson.

———. 1994. *Symbol and Magic in Egyptian Art*. London: Thames and Hudson.

———. 2000. *The Complete Temples of Ancient Egypt*. London: Thames and Hudson.

———. 2003. *The Complete Gods and Goddesses of Ancient Egypt*. London: Thames and Hudson.

Zakrezewski, S. R. 2003. "Variations in Ancient Egyptian Stature and Body Proportions." *American Journal of Physical Anthropology* 121: 219–229.

Acknowledgments

This book has long been in planning as a guide to one of the most popular Kelsey Museum objects and arises, in part, from one of our most frequently asked questions—what does the Djehutymose coffin say? I began to translate its texts over a decade ago in my Advanced Middle Egyptian course, and I'd like to thank my students from various offerings of the class, especially Alec Robinette, Belgin Elbs, Lindsay Ambridge, Tom Landvatter, Sarah Oas, and Jessie Roy, for their hard work and enthusiasm. More immediate impetus for the book came from the new photographs of the coffin, taken by University Library photographer Randal Stegmeyer prior to its installation in the new Upjohn Exhibit Wing of the Kelsey Museum. These photographs led me to feature the Djehutymose coffin in my undergraduate course "Ancient Egypt: Religion and Culture," and the resulting class lectures provided the framework for this book. So thanks are also due to Randal Stegmeyer for his wonderful images, and to my students—I'm particularly indebted to Kevin Noelke and Luke Reyhl for their encouragement and thoughtful comments on the manuscript for this book.

The Kelsey Museum is a small community in which everyone pitches in, and I've benefitted greatly from the support of this environment. Special thanks to Kelsey Museum Coordinator of Museum Collections Sebastián Encina for coordinating photo sessions for the Djehutymose coffin and related objects, as well as pulling together archival database photographs of museum objects. Scott Meier, Michelle Fontenot, Suzanne Davis, and Claudia Chemello conserved, handled, and moved objects for the various photographic sessions and provided other essential help. Other photographs were contributed by John Kannenberg, Janet Richards, and Carrie Roberts, while Todd Gerring supplied essential mummy-making materials and other assistance. Thanks to Hans Anderson for permission to use a still from his video featuring images from the coffin and Paula Metzner of the Kalamazoo Valley Museum for a wonderful historic photograph of the coffin on display in Kalamazoo. Thanks also to Patrick Shea for help with the image of Albert M. Todd from the Chemical Heritage Foundation Collections. Maps are adapted from a base map by Lorene Sterner.

Djehutymose maintains a lively online presence, thanks to the talents of Kelsey Museum docent Marlene Goldsmith, and I thank her for her hard work, and also her great enthusiasm and encouragement on this book. Laurie Talalay has been a crucial source of help and support through the writing of this book, and I thank her, as well as Kelsey director Sharon Herbert and fellow curators Elaine Gazda and Margaret Root. The Kelsey Museum of Archaeology is a part of the College of Literature, Science, and the Arts at the University of Michigan; the College is a generous and encouraging supporter of the Kelsey Museum, and I've benefitted from College research funding in a variety of ways during the writing of this book.

Kelsey Museum editor Peg Lourie shaped the manuscript into the finished volume, and I'd like to thank her for her careful design and editing, patience and good cheer. Carl Abrego and Sandra Malveaux keep Kelsey Museum Publications going, and I appreciate all their hard work for this book. Thanks to Janet Richards for temporarily taking over as our series editor and arranging the refereeing of this book.

My work on Djehutymose's coffin started from Jonathan Elias' discussion of the coffin and its parallels in his 1993 doctoral dissertation, and I am deeply indebted to this careful, meticulous work. Maarten Raven, of the Rijksmuseum van Oudheden in Leiden, generously gave me much useful information about the Kelsey Museum Ptah-Sokar-Osiris figures. I owe a great debt of thanks to the three anonymous referees for this book for their time and effort in making helpful comments and corrections. Any errors that remain are my own.

My friends always support my writing, and I'd like to thank Andrew Ferrara, Margie Fisher, Chris Hinson, Adam Hyatt, John Kannenberg, Chet McLeskey, Carl Nyman, and Gina Soter for getting me through the process of writing and revising this book. Thanks especially to Greg Madden, friend and constant reader, for specific comments on the manuscript, as well as all his encouragement and help over the years.

Finally, I would like to thank my friend and colleague Janet Richards, first of all for generously ceding her rights to publish the Djehutymose coffin and related material, for allowing me to use her part of the Kelsey collection for illustrative material, and for her thoughtful and enthusiastic comments on the manuscript of this book. In gratitude for all her support, encouragement, and friendship during our time at the Kelsey Museum, I dedicate this book to her.

Photo Credits

Randall Stegmeyer
1–2, 4–5, 18–30, 36, 38, 40–41, 43–50, 54–59, 62–63, 65–75, 78–81, 84–89, 91–96, 98, 100–105, 107–109, 112, 114–117, 119–120, 122–125, 130–134, 137–141, 143–144, 146–147, 149, 152–158, 160, front cover, back cover

Kelsey Museum file photographs
3, 8–14, 16–17, 31–35, 37, 39, 42, 60–61, 64, 76–77, 82–83, 90, 97, 99, 106, 110–111, 113, 121, 126–129, 135–136, 142, 145, 148, 151, 163

Hans Anderson
165

Chemical Heritage Foundation Collections
159

R. J. Cook for the University of Michigan Abydos Middle Cemetery Project
150

Sebastián Encina
164, 168, back cover flap

Kalamazoo Valley Museum
162

John Kannenberg
118, 167

Carrie Roberts
161

T. G. Wilfong
6–7, 53, 166